JEREMY LIN
From the End of the Bench to Stardom

An Unauthorized Biography by
Bill Davis

ISBN 978-0-9853343-0-7

Printed in the U.S.A.

Table of Contents

To all the underdogs
who never did
get the chance
to succeed.

CHAPTER ONE
The Early Years

"Players don't usually come out of nowhere. If you can go back and take a look, [Jeremy Lin's] skill level was probably there from the beginning..."

—Kobe Bryant, February 10, 2012

The summer of 1988 was unusually sweltering. A heat wave had launched a full-court press on the city of Los Angeles, California. Summer traffic took Wilshire and Sunset boulevards hostage, mobs of tourists trampled the star-studded Hollywood streets, and bodybuilders flexed and released on the boardwalks of Venice Beach.

The heat, however, was not the only anomaly that summer. The Los Angeles Dodgers were having a miraculous baseball season. Led by Orel Hershiser and Kirk Gibson, the Dodgers were wrapping up a wildly successful August with a 17-12 record, following June in which the team went 17-9. The underdog Dodgers would go on to defeat the heavily favored New York Mets for the National League Championship. Then they would face the Oakland Athletics in the World Series, beating them

4 games to 1. Hershiser's success wasn't sudden, but it was surprising because he was smaller than most major league baseball players. Despite what could have been a setback, Hershiser's uncompromising work ethic and focus on the basics gave him the edge he needed. Two decades later, this same idea would hold true for a certain Asian-American athlete who would take the world by storm. For now, Hershiser was grabbing headlines throughout the country. It was the season of the Underdog, when it felt like anything could happen. It was as if there was something in the air.

A few miles from Dodger Stadium, Gie-Ming and Shirley Lin were welcoming their second child into the world. Jeremy Shu-How Lin was born on August 23, 1988.[1] For his parents, who were Taiwanese immigrants, their son seemed to represent the American Dream – both a symbol of its possibilities and a reminder that hard work will ensure a bright future. Jeremy's presence brought the Lin brood up to four. His older brother, Josh, was born in 1987.[2] About five years later, his brother Joseph would join the Lin family. There were now five players for the Lin squad, enough to form a team of their own.

In fact, throughout Jeremy's life, his family – namely his parents – would become and remain his most important teammates. As Fu-Chang Lo, a member of Lin's family church, told *The New York Times*, "Jeremy's life was formed by his parents."[3] Throughout the many stories of Lin's rise, there is one notion that is certain – there would be no "Linsanity" without Lin's parents. While his father inspired in Jeremy a love for the game and helped hone his skills, Jeremy's mother coached her son's work ethic and helped create new opportunities for Jeremy to play basketball.[4]

Gie-Ming Lin – Jeremy's father – was born in the early 1950s in Beidou, Taiwan. During Gie-Ming's childhood, Taiwan was a one-party state ruled under martial law. Even without much freedom, Gie-Ming fought to get an education. Being a great student was a family tradition – his father and grandfather before him were unusually learned men.[5] And so he charted a path to National Taiwan University, the "Harvard" of Taiwan. After graduation, an NTU-alumnus, Ping Tcheng, then a professor at Old Dominion University in Norfolk, Virginia, was looking for an engineering research assistant. He offered Gie-Ming the position.[6]

In 1977, Gie-Ming Lin left Taiwan for Norfolk, Virginia.[7] His emigration to America was not only for academic and career opportunities. Whether knowingly or not, Gie-Ming embarked on a journey that had been

4

years in the making, spurred by a sport he had witnessed only a handful of times. But even on those rare occasions, it was evident Gie-Ming had fallen in love with basketball.[8] As Jeremy Lin told *ESPN*'s Dana O'Neil in 2009, "My dad is a complete basketball junkie."[9]

For years, Jeremy's father had hoped that he would journey to the birthplace of basketball. As Gie-Ming admits, a research assistant position and the desire to earn a master's degree were not his only motivators for moving to the States. He wanted "to watch the NBA."[10] Soon after he arrived in the United States, Gie-Ming began recording NBA games and the players who inspired him.[11] Over time he would collect hours upon hours of footage of the legends themselves – players like Julius Erving and Moses Malone[12], who was awarded the NBA's MVP award at age 23.[13]

In part, it was this love of basketball that set him on a path that would lead him to his life's greatest love, his wife Shirley. At Old Dominion, Gie-Ming met Xinxin Wu, (who became known as Shirley upon arrival in Virginia). She was a beautiful, computer-science student.[14] From Kaohsiung, Taiwan, Shirley was a sweet, no-nonsense academic as stunning as she was smart.[15] The couple soon fell in love. After Gie-Ming completed his master's degree in mechanical engineering in December

1979, he and Shirley moved to Purdue University, where the two continued their studies.[16] After the couple completed their degrees – Gie-Ming earned a doctorate in computer science – they followed various work opportunities around the country before settling in Ranchos Palos Verdes, California in 1985.[17]

It was during this time, living in a suburb of Los Angeles, that Gie-Ming was looking for a way to unwind from the stress and strains of work.[18] "I thought it would be great to play basketball," Gie-Ming recalled of the time.[19] As O'Neil reported for *ESPN*[20]:

"Only problem? He didn't have the slightest idea how. He had never picked up a ball in his life. So he turned his attention back to those gripping NBA games. Armed with videotapes of his favorite players, Gie-Ming studied the game with the same fervor he studied for his Ph.D. 'I would just imitate them over and over; I got my hook shot from Kareem,' Gie-Ming said, laughing."

Soon, Gie-Ming was practicing regularly at the local YMCA. At the time it was a simple, somewhat small sports-club near the Lin home. The gymnasium was spacious and lively, but unassuming. Dull colors gilded the walls. The court was scuffed with sneaker marks. The balls were worn and faded – it was impossible to decipher the Spalding's from the Wilson's. These days, the complex is more modern. The north façade now doubles as a rock-climbing wall. Air balls – with pristine manufacturer logos intact - constantly peg the "boulders" on the wall. The court's buffed surface shimmers. Once a site of the commonplace, the arena has become a place of notoriety. After all, this is where Jeremy most likely took his first three-pointer, or where he executed his first give-and-go. Now there is an aura of excitement about the gymnasium. It plays like an "Eighth Wonder of the World" in Palo Alto. The backboards, rims, and floorboards seem sacred.

At the time, however, it was a simple classroom. First, Gie-Ming entered as a student. He continued to hone his skills and even started to partake in some pick-up games. A few years later, after the births of his three sons, he became a teacher. It was in 1992 that Gie-Ming first brought his oldest son Joshua to the YMCA to practice drills. Josh was five years old at the time. A couple of years later Jeremy joined in on the action, and then Joseph a few years after.[21]

The Gie-Ming-led practice sessions became a tri-weekly event. Homework had to be completed and dinner gulped down before trekking across town to play ball.[22] The elder Lin focused on the basics. "I realized if I brought them from a young age it would be like second nature for them," Gie-Ming told *ESPN*.[23] "If they had the fundamentals, the rest would be easy."[24] The drills were tedious. Yet the boys loved every minute. Their joy, commitment, and enchantment with the sport were contagious.

These basketball clinics were among the most cherished memories the boys shared with their father. Basketball became a pastime for the Lins. It placed up there with the family's love of fishing. In embracing the American sport of basketball, it was as if the Lins had finally established their place in the community, and in a larger sense, the country. It was a testament that the American Dream was alive and well within Joshua's, Jeremy's and Joseph's spirits.

Gie-Ming's efforts to develop his sons' talents echoed the efforts of other fathers of professional athletes. Tiger Woods' father, Earl, began priming Tiger for a career in golf before the child prodigy reached the age of two. Richard Williams, the father of Venus and Serena, coached his daughters vigorously throughout their teens. Michael Jordan's father, James R. Jordan, Sr., was equally as involved with his son's training. But Gie-

Ming's story stands alone. While many of these father coaches were athletes in their own right, Gie-Ming only learned the fundamentals of the game a few years before he taught his sons. It was not about athleticism, though he was certainly athletic. It was more about perseverance and the capacity to learn. Gie-Ming's ability to teach his sons the game of basketball so successfully shows that we can achieve anything we put our minds to. Perhaps it was this lesson that resonated so deeply with Joshua, Jeremy, and Joseph.

Gie-Ming Lin was not the only parent to impart an example of excellence onto his children. Jeremy's mother, Shirley was an equal partner in Jeremy's path to basketball stardom. It is rare to hear stories about a mother of an athlete being so intimately involved in her child's craft. Sure, most athletes will give credit for their success to their mothers – all of those hours of driving, late-night pep talks, unconditional love, good morals, etc. But we do not hear much about the mothers who understand techniques of the sport or the analytics of the game. Shirley Wu was a powerhouse in that respect. She built up an uncanny knowledge of the game and was a tremendous asset for Jeremy. Aside from being a common fixture and vocal supporter at games, Shirley would "[organize] rides to games" and "[print] out statistics of upcoming opponents."[25] Shirley was the driving force behind starting an advanced basketball program for elementary school-aged students, when Jeremy was of the age. Thanks to Shirley's efforts, a National Junior Basketball program was created in Palo Alto, California.[26] Jeremy's mother also insisted that schoolwork came first. So long as Jeremy kept up his grades, he was allowed to play basketball.[27] She reinforced the idea that a successful person should have both a strong mind and a strong body. Academics were as important as athletics.

Although Shirley worked full-time, her devotion to her children was unmatched. In Jeremy's case, Shirley made his passion her passion. She took part in educating herself about the game her son loved so much. She concentrated her time and efforts in making him as successful at this sport as possible. She worked tirelessly to take advantage of existing opportunities and create new avenues for Jeremy to hone his skills. She championed her son and his talents simply because basketball was something that Jeremy loved so dearly. She inspired Jeremy to believe that he could achieve anything he wished. Lin's high school coach and long-time mentor, Peter Diepenbrock, credits Shirley with Lin's successful spirit. As he told *ESPN*'s Tim Keown, "'You know how parents tell their kids they can do anything? Most people just say it to say it, but Jeremy's mom *lives* it. Because of that, Jeremy's always had this ridiculous confidence level.'"[28]

Shirley also encouraged Jeremy to continue playing basketball during the summers. In fifth grade Jeremy enrolled in a basketball camp in Palo Alto. It was here that he met Diepenbrock, who was helping to run the program. Little did Jeremy know that this man would later change his life. Even during Jeremy's elementary school years, Diepenbrock noticed something exceptional in him. As Diepenbrock told *The Daily Beast*, "Obviously [Jeremy] was very, very small, but a very good player – very good instincts, very good feel – and his leadership stuck out."[29] He would later have the privilege of coaching Lin at Palo Alto High School.

But first it was off to middle school for Jeremy. He enrolled at Jane Lathrop Stanford Middle School in Palo Alto and in his first year tried out for the school's basketball team.[30] He was a scrawny kid with an intense spirit.

By the time he reached eighth grade, Jeremy's talent drew attention. Rick Chandler, who coached Jeremy during that 2001-2002 season, remembers the impression he made at the school. Chandler recalls the school's athletic director, Mike Ferolino, telling him during tryouts, "So there's this kid Jeremy Lin, and you're not going to have to watch him very much. He's about the best player we've ever had here; he's going right to the A team."[31] In his column for NBC Sports, Chandler – now a reporter – recalls how Jeremy initially failed to stand out. Soon, however, "his game came into focus, and he was doing things that eighth graders aren't supposed to be able to do. Lin saw everything two moves ahead – something so rare for middle schoolers...Toward the end of the first day, when Lin whipped a behind-the-back pass toward open air – only to have a teammate appear at the last second to catch it and take two steps in for a layin – I had seen enough," Chandler wrote.[32] In an interview with the *North Lake Tahoe Bonanza*, Chandler elaborated on Lin's rareness. "He is one of the few players I've coached who came to me almost fully formed," Chandler said. "His grasp of the fundamentals was so far and away above the other players' that it just kind of amazed me, because in eighth grade you usually have to start from scratch."[33] Chandler couldn't have known it at the time, but what he saw in Jeremy was a result of Gie-Ming's and Shirley's efforts all of those years. Jeremy's exceptional foundation was no fluke – it was the product of years of practice and hard work.

Jeremy's early years set the stage for his future success. Throughout this period Jeremy honed his basketball skills. His tri-weekly "basketball nights" with his father were undoubtedly a monumental beginning. So too were the hours of practice and regulation games for both school teams and private, advanced squads. These hours upon hours of work and development were instrumental. Jeremy was maturing as a player in terms of both technical skills and game strategy. But perhaps more importantly, Jeremy was developing a rich work ethic and showed unyielding effort. Even in these early stages, there was something special about Jeremy. He had a level of commitment and expertise that was unique for children his age. His coaches, friends, friends' parents, and others in their community noticed it.

Above all else, Jeremy's early years were shaped by his family's meaningful teachings. He began to showcase qualities of teamwork, humility, drive, and devotion both on and off the court. He applied the lessons he learned in the Lin family home to his basketball games. And vice versa. Ever present were the markings of Gie-Ming and Shirley's influences. They were magnetically positive and powerful. Couple that with Jeremy's ability to work hard and tackle challenges, and you had a recipe for success.

Years later, as a Harvard senior, Jeremy would have this to say about his parents:

"My dad has been a very special person in my life obviously and he has shown me the way and he is the reason why I got into basketball. And I want to include my mom on this. I just think I look up to my parents because when we talk about basketball, they don't necessarily talk always about whether we won or whether we scored a lot of points. I think they do a great job of teaching me about playing in a Godly manner. I think there will be times where I might have a great individual performance but I might lose my temper and that's what they're going to talk to me about...I'm still learning from them. The way they see the game and the way they judge me on the court is more valuable than anything else they can do."[34]

In the past few weeks, commentators, reporters, and pundits alike have classified the 6-foot, 3-inch superstar as an overnight success who "came out of nowhere." His early life, however, shows this is not really true. Instead, his success developed over the course of many nights: First, three nights a week at the YMCA and, later, on game nights at Jane Lathrop Stanford Middle School.

After middle school, the nocturnal contests were

just heating up. Jeremy wished to continue his path to success in high school. The only question was what kind of an impact Jeremy would have at Palo Alto High School. Clocking in around 5 feet tall with a shot that originated from below the hip, Jeremy's success as a high school player was uncertain. It would be another summer of practice, fishing, and In-N-Out burgers – Jeremy's favorite – before his high school career would begin. Only this summer, the summer of 2002, things were a little different.

There was no longer a heat wave this summer. The temperature remained somewhat cool. But although it wasn't sweltering, as Jeremy prepared for his first year of high school, there still seemed to be something special in the air.

It's a terrific story, [Jeremy] seems like a wonderful young man, and it elevates this great sport all around the world.

— **President Barack Obama**

CHAPTER TWO
The High School Years

The halls of Palo Alto High School – or "Paly," as it's known in the neighborhood – seemed eerily quiet in mid-August. The final days of the summer of 2002 ushered in eager anticipation throughout the vacant building. The quad awaited the stampede of students; the buses begged for company; the lockers longed to be decoded. The school was a stone's throw away from Stanford University. Paly loomed in the shadow of the "Harvard of the West." The college served as a constant source of inspiration for the high school students.

For many, it was a dream that seemed close enough to reach. And an education at Palo Alto High School provided ample opportunity to make that dream a reality. After all, Paly was well known for encouraging high academic achievement – its students scored well on SAT and AP exams and achieved national success in debate, science research, and mathematics. But academic rigor was valued alongside the arts and athletics. Theater, music, and writing flourished at the school, as did its sports programs.

The campus was admired for both its standardized excellence as well as its quirks, which usually came in the form of its annual senior pranks. (In the late 1990s, for example, a group of seniors let loose six hamsters during an AP Biology exam.) It was no wonder, then, that this academic and extracurricular laboratory served as alma mater for Olympians and film actors, novelists and rock stars, artists and even a U.S. Senator. No one could predict it at the time, but Paly High was about to welcome to its ranks another of its most notable future alumni.

At the end of August, the first day of the 2002-2003 school year welcomed a new crop of Paly Vikings. Among them was a 14-year-old named Jeremy. The freshman didn't have to duck his head as he passed under the Spanish-style, red roof and entered the doors of his new school. Backpack in tow, Lin was only 5 feet and 3 inches tall, with a scrawny frame to match.

The greens and whites (Paly's school colors) splashed across lockers and water fountains, corridors and bulletin boards, must have seemed foreign to Jeremy at first. His older brother, Joshua, had taken refuge in the blacks and reds of Henry M. Gunn High School where he had played both junior varsity and varsity basketball. In fact, when Joshua played JV ball, Jeremy volunteered as scorekeeper at his games. When Joshua graduated to playing varsity, Jeremy would mirror the team's practice drills somewhere off-court.[1] But Jeremy felt that his brother didn't get the playing opportunities he deserved with the Gunn Titans.[2] And while this wasn't a reason for

Jeremy to enroll at Palo Alto High School, it certainly made it more exciting when starting fresh with a new basketball program.

That fall, however, Jeremy did not make the varsity squad. While it may have been crushing, Lin could find comfort in knowing that his idol – Michael Jordan – failed to make his varsity basketball team as a *sophomore* at Emsley A. Laney High School in Wilmington, North Carolina. Just as Jordan became the star of his junior varsity team, so too did Lin. His performances on the court were electric. His teammates looked to his leadership and skill-set for each and every play. His freshman coach would later toast Lin at the team banquet, saying, "Jeremy has a better skill set than anyone I've ever seen at his age."[3]

Jeremy was a big fish in a small pond, and yearned for the chance to play varsity ball. His wishes would be answered that spring, as the Paly Vikings entered the playoffs. Coach Diepenbrock recruited Jeremy to play for varsity in the play-off opener. The Vikings had become state champions 10 years prior in 1993 and the team sought to honor that tradition. But many people were hesitant for Jeremy to enter the "big leagues" because of his small size. "He was so small, a buddy called and said, 'He's going to get hurt out there,'" Diepenbrock recalled.[4] Still, Diepenbrock played Lin in the opener against Yerba Buena of the Blossom Valley Athletic League. The Vikings won 63-44. The team's 17-9 record that year was no fluke. But, as *The Campanile*, Paly's school newspaper, wrote at the time, "the biggest story was…freshman call-up Jeremy Lin, who made his first three shots with Varsity, all three-pointers, after recently being recruited from Junior Varsity for the playoffs."[5]

The Vikings went on to beat Saint Francis of the West Catholic Athletic League before heading to the Central Coast Section (CCS) Final Four.[6] The Vikings soon defeated Woodside High School in the semifinals and Aragon High School in the championship game. When the team returned home to Palo Alto they received a hero's welcome.[7]

But the section title was not the only thing that had people back home talking. Jeremy's prowess on the court – in spite of his size – was heavily noticed. The Asian-American, who had a poster of Latrell Sprewell in his bedroom[8] and who donned Nike Shox BB4's,[9] was now a known entity in the high school basketball scene. His promotion to varsity would be permanent. Still, he cherished his time on the JV team, which was wildly successful. For his efforts that year, he earned the Team MVP and All-League MVP awards which he shared with teammate Cooper Miller.[10]

Sophomore year presented a time of new opportunity for Lin. Now playing for the varsity, Jeremy was deemed a "player to watch" by the Paly student newspaper before the season had even commenced.[11] His first full year on the varsity was to be "good, but not great."[12] Though consistent, he was not yet a stand out. The Viking point guard failed to make a splash in the January 7th game against Fremont and again in the January 9th contest with the Milpitas Trojans.[13]

His first notables that season seemed to come in the form of three-point shots against the Santa Clara Bruins. The first shot put the Vikings on the scoreboard, while the second capped off a 15-point run in the second quarter.[14] At the end of the fourth quarter, the Vikings had claimed victory. While the spotlight wasn't focused on Lin, the Vikings had rallied an impressive 25-3 record going into the playoffs. Perhaps the lack of focus on Jeremy was more a testament to the strengths of the team as a whole. As Lin said at the time, "We're composed of players who are used to being stars on their respective teams, but this year we've done a great job coming together and accepting our roles."[15]

The Paly community might have caught its first glimpse of "Linsanity" during the Vikings' final regular-season game against its chief rival – the Gunn Titans. The Vikings had destroyed the Titans 52-33 in their previous game, but the February 12 contest proved to be a different ball game.[16] By halftime the Titans led the Vikings by 4 points, a lead which expanded to 7 in the fourth quarter, with just four minutes left. There seemed to be a certain energy ignited in the team's Asian-American point guard. With minutes to go, the Vikings executed a 10-0 run to lead the Titans 49-46 and ensure victory in the emotionally charged game. But something had just happened in that gymnasium. The skinny Asian kid had unleashed a tour de force against his opponents. *The Campanile* captured the moment:

"Lin scored eight of the team's final 10 points to lead the comeback. He hit a key three-pointer to tie the game at 46 points; seconds later, after stealing the basketball, he was fouled and made two free throws to give Paly a 48-46 lead. He added another free throw with 8.7 seconds remaining to guarantee the victory."[17]

From there, the Vikings advanced to the CCS play-offs, facing the Santa Clara Bruins on February 25. Lin commanded an impressive steal and 3-pointer in the second quarter, while offering up an alleyoop to teammate Brian Baskauskas in the third. He finished the game with 9 points. The Vikings beat the Bruins 58-45, advancing to the CCS quarterfinals.[18] But the streak did not last long.

The Vikings' bid for a second straight CCS championship was over almost as quickly as it began. In the CCS quarterfinals the Vikings eventually fell to North Salinas High school, in a devastating overtime loss of 53-52.[19] The game was a disappointment for the team, and a blow to Lin personally. His first full year on the varsity had not ended as he would have hoped. But the season provided an excellent learning opportunity for the young man. He was able to hone his skills, develop his instincts, and log hundreds of hours of practice and playing time.

Jeremy's growth as a player was also complimented by physical changes. He had been getting taller and started to fill out. Gie-Ming remembers that during sophomore year, Jeremy was able to dunk for the first time. "He came to tell me, 'Daddy, I can dunk!' I said, 'Are you sure?'" Gie-Ming mused to Sports Illustrated.[20] But the end of the season now offered a new beginning for Jeremy. He won high accolades for his season, taking home the Sophomore of the Year award. With a foundation of success behind him, the following season would catapult Lin into a new position; he would soon be an upperclassman on the team, and would be expected to provide leadership on and off the court.

Although the season was over, Jeremy was enjoying high school. The middle Lin child was well liked at Paly and was deeply involved in both academics and extra-curricular life. Schoolwork was a priority for Jeremy, who excelled in all subjects, especially the sciences. And while the drive to succeed in the classroom was self-established, his mother took no chances in having basketball get in the way. When Jeremy had an A-minus average or below in a particular class, Shirley informed Coach Diepenbrock that unless the grade improved, Jeremy would have to sit out a game or a practice.[21] Still, Jeremy's academic prowess was undeniable. As Coach Diepenbrock would later acknowledge in an interview with *The Daily Beast*, "Jeremy was a great student. He would have gotten into Harvard whether he was a good basketball player or not. He just had the incredible ability to basically structure his life and organize himself and make sure that he had his priorities straight. I think that with every individual, discipline level off the court translates directly to [one's] discipline level on the court."[22]

Jeremy also took part in the extra-curricular organizations that Palo Alto High School had to offer. He became a contributing sports writer for *The Campanile*, the student newspaper, covering a variety of sports including baseball, volleyball, and cross-country.[23]

Perhaps Jeremy's most important affiliation was as a member of the Paly Christian Club. The student-run organization served as a perfect blend of community and religion. Here, Jeremy could participate in community service, organize faith-based outreach events, and socialize with friends, all in the name of God. For Jeremy, this proved a true love. He even became co-president of the organization his senior year.[24]

Jeremy's faith played a vital role in his life – its tenets served as guideposts for him along his incredible journey. A devout Evangelical Christian, Jeremy grew up attending church regularly with his family. He was ever present in the Sunday morning pews. But his relationship with the Church didn't end there.

On Friday nights, Jeremy and his brothers would attend "youth gatherings" at the Chinese Church in Christ where they would study with the pastor Stephen Chen. Afterwards, the three Lin boys and Chen would head to play basketball, sometimes into the wee hours of the night, before finishing the night off with a trip to Denny's or In-N-Out Burger.[25]

Even Lin's approach to basketball was coated in religious ideas, as championed by his parents. Daniel Burke of the *Religion News Service* explains how "Lin... credits his parents with teaching him to play 'godly basketball,' which measures success by sportsmanship, not stats. That means putting teammates first and showing respect to opponents and referees."[26] Jeremy would pray before each basketball game, a practice he continues before his NBA games as well. Faith and basketball went together for Jeremy.

The summer of 2004 soon arrived, and even sooner departed. Its passing transformed Jeremy into a junior at Palo Alto High School. Anticipation for the season was ripe. Jeremy was now well known, which meant more exposure and opportunity. With opportunity, however, came many challenges which colored the start of the season in an unfortunate way.

Jeremy had grown considerably, but opponents and onlookers still discounted his abilities at first glance. His race had much to do with the other teams' discrimination. "Sometimes, other players would call me a 'Chinese import' and different names. When we would line up for the ball, the other team's point guard and shooting guard would argue over who would guard me, because they both wanted to," Lin told *Dime Magazine* in 2009.[27]

The racist taunts and underestimation continued throughout the years. Ignorant individuals would make snide remarks, cruelly taunting Lin both on and off the court. It was his father, Gie-Ming, who perhaps imparted the most important guidance. As Gie-Ming told *ESPN*, "I told [Jeremy] people are going to say things to him, but he had to stay calm and not get excited by these words; they are only words. I told him to just win the game for your school and people will respect you."[28]

Besides, Lin's talent on the hardwood was enough to silence most detractors. Viking teammate Brad Lehman recalls, "Yeah people underestimated him initially, until about two minutes into the game when they realized he was faster and could shoot, drive and do everything. I think they were just surprised that this little skinny Asian kid was just going off on them."[29]

And "go off on them" he did. Throughout his junior season, Lin completely dominated games. The Vikings seemed unstoppable with Jeremy's game changing 3-pointers, no-look passes, and powerful drives. Paly started to rack up the wins. It won three major tournaments – the Gator Classic, the Half Moon Bay tournament, and the Maui Christmas Classic Tournament Championship – before the season even kicked into full gear.[3031] The team devastated the Gunn Titans 69-27[32], and overcame Woodside High School in an overtime nail-biter.[33] Coverage of the miraculous season always flaunted Lin's brilliance. His "acrobatic pull-up three-point jump shot"[34] and his "thunderous two-handed breakaway dunk" became the stuff of legend.[35]

Of course, Lin would be the first to argue that it was truly a team effort. And in reality, it was. The Vikings quickly ascended through the CCS, beating the Lincoln High School Lions in the first round, surpassing the Evergreen Valley Cougars in the second, and trampling Sequoia High School in the semi-finals.[36] The Vikings were set to play the Mitty High School Monarchs of San Jose in the CCS final at San Jose State University.

The night before the game, however, Coach Diepenbrock got a call. It was Jeremy. He had broken his ankle playing a pick-up game at the YMCA.[37] The same YMCA where Gie-Ming had trained with him all those years prior. The same YMCA that had been his entrance to the game he loved, but now represented the end of Jeremy's season. Diepenbrock thought he was kidding. But Jeremy would never kid about something like that.

Sadly, Jeremy traded in his white and green uniform for a t-shirt and jeans, as he sat on the sidelines to cheer on his team. He watched as his Vikings beat the Monarchs for the CCS Championship, then the Chico

High School Panthers in the Northern California Division II State Semi-finals.[38] But Lin's injured status may have sealed Paly's fate in its loss against Oak Ridge High School, as the team lost the NorCal finals and failed to advance to the California State Championship game.[39]

The loss was devastating for the team that went 31-2, but especially for Jeremy. If only he hadn't played that pick-up game at the Y, if only he hadn't broken his ankle, perhaps he would have led his team to a state championship. But the carelessness that led to the injury was not just a random accident.

Although Jeremy had delivered stellar performances on the court, his attitude off it had been much less positive. Lin explains his state of mind best. When asked about his biggest obstacle growing up, Lin told the *New York Daily News*, "I want to just say when I broke my ankle my junior year. It was the night before the championship game. That changed my whole life because before that, up to that point, I was a really bad practice player, I had a lot of attitude, I'd be kicked out of practice. I just wouldn't listen to any of the coaches. I felt like I was just the best player. And once I broke my ankle it changed my whole perspective. On everything. I just told myself, 'I don't know how long I'm going to be able to play because at any minute you can lose your career, and while I play, as many days as God gives me, I'm going to make sure I go 100 percent.'"[40]

The injury was a revelation for Jeremy. His subsequent acknowledgment of his actions and his commitment to change his attitude showed a unique level of maturity for a sixteen year old. Lin's injury had caused him to think deeply about basketball and being able to do what he loved. And through this reflection, Jeremy had settled into his role as a true, tested leader. His captainship senior year was both a testament to his impressive personal character as well as his domination on the court. Lin was now determined to take his team to the State Championship. It would be his last chance.

This season was all about getting off on the right foot – or the right "ankle" in Lin's case. In pre-season, Coach Diepenbrock "sat his star player down and said, 'Let's tell it like it is. I'm the defensive coordinator; you're the offensive coordinator. Just get it done.'"[41] It was now Jeremy's time to lead. But the captain recognized the team's greatest asset – its effortless teamwork.

The squad boasted six stellar senior players – Lin, Kheaton Scott, Steven Brown, Cooper Miller, Brad Lehman, and Kevin Trimble – who had played together since elementary school. They could anticipate each other's rhythms and instincts. As Diepenbrock told *The*

Campanile in 2006, "'An opposing coach told me that teams can play whole seasons and never hope to have the sort of team chemistry that we have already. But [the chemistry] seems to be a natural thing; it comes from having six seniors who have played together for a long time.'"[42] It would be the team-focused approach that Lin cherished most, a far cry from the individual stat-based play in the NBA's D-League some years later.

But for now, the Vikings were off to an impressive season. They cruised to victory in two preseason tournaments – the James Lick Tournament and the Santa Cruz Dads Club Tournament.[43] The team followed by going 7-0 in non-league match-ups.[44] In league play, the Vikings handily defeated their opponents. Aside from their loss against Division-V champion Price High School, the Vikings were undefeated, squelching Paso Robles, Fremont, Mountain View, and Gunn twice, among other schools.[45] In the CCS playoffs, Lin took over, scoring 33 points in the first round against Woodside, and carrying the team with 19 points in the CCS Finals against the Archbishop Mitty Monarchs.[46]

The NorCal playoffs would prove to be a different beast, but the team easily rose to the challenge. In the first round, the Vikings blew past the Richmond Oilers handing them an easy defeat. Next up were the Laguna

Creek Cardinals. With a minute to go in regulation time, and the score tied, Lin turned on the magic, nailing a crucial 3-pointer and a no-look pass to Brown whose jump shot sealed the win for the Vikings.

Diepenbrock's crew took to the NorCal finals, facing the Mitty Monarchs. After a disappointing first quarter – the Monarchs led 20-6 – the Vikings quickly recovered. While the Monarchs double-teamed Lin in the final minutes of the game, the senior point guard executed two crucial assists to Brad Lehman, whose 3-pointers gave the Vikings the win.[47]

The Vikings were now slated to face the Mater Dei Monarchs, the Southern California (SoCal) champions. The match-up had the makings of a true David vs. Goliath story. For just like in the Biblical tale, size kept the Vikings at a major disadvantage. Mater Dei had eight players who clocked in at 6-foot-7 or taller[48], including 7-foot-1 Alex Jacobson.

The Vikings, on the other hand, had no one taller than 6-6, and Kheaton Scott as their center at 6 feet.[49] Similarly, the Monarchs had greater numbers, athleticism, and even talent. But if there was one constant in Jeremy Lin's life, it was that he consistently defied expectations. That fighting spirit spread to the rest of the Paly teens, who became inspired by their disadvantage and rose to the challenge.

This was the game that Jeremy had been waiting for, the biggest game that he had ever played. For over a year, the Asian-American point guard sought to redeem himself from his undisciplined injury. His steals, back door passes, and jump shots overtook the game. With 2:07 on the clock on a two-point lead, Jeremy "connected on a desperation 25-foot bank shot from the top of the key as the 35-second buzzer sounded."[50] As Mater Dei Coach Gary McKnight told *The Los Angeles Times*, "[That] bank shot broke our back."[51]

The Vikings shot more consistently, hustled harder, and connected seamlessly. Their 51-47 upset over Mater Dei was a true victory and a wonderful pinnacle for Jeremy's Paly basketball career. "Nobody would have ever dreamed that we could come out on top in the state. But it was reality tonight," Lin told *The Paly Voice* at the time.[52]

The newly minted California Division II State Champions were grateful for their captain. Yes, he had scored 17 points and finished with 8 rebounds.[53] But it was his leadership that his teammates most respected, a brand of leadership that seemed otherworldly. Years later, in an interview, Coach Diepenbrock would revisit Jeremy's skill as a leader. "To me, leadership is the ability to say things to your teammates or to others without regard to consequences, and that's really who [Jeremy] is. Jeremy would just say whatever it took to get the job done, and the guys respected that and followed him. He was always spot on as far as what needed to be done on the basketball court," Diepenbrock recalled.[54]

Lin finished the season as the team's Most Valuable Player. He dominated every stat category and averaged 16 points, 5 rebounds, 7 assists, and 4 steals per game.[55] He also garnered boys' basketball Northern California Division II Player of the Year, Northern California Scholar Athlete of the Year, and First Team All-State recognition, and was named the San Francisco Chronicle's basketball Player of the Year.[56] Jeremy Lin had quickly become Palo Alto's golden child. His hard work and unrivaled devotion had paid off. It was a moment of sheer bliss for Lin and his family. He took to the school's newspaper, *The Campanile*, to articulate his thoughts and share his thanks. The letter – reproduced, in part below – offers an intimate portrait of Jeremy's thoughts:

"As I look back and reflect upon my four-year basketball career here at Palo Alto High School, I realize how perfectly everything worked out. Before this year, winning a state championship was a stretch of my imagination. After that goal became reality, my natural tendency was to give myself the credit for the win. However, the more I think about the experience, the more I understand that I deserve less and less credit. I realize I could have done absolutely nothing without the support of so many other people, and I want to take this opportunity to express my gratitude. First off, I want to thank God for guiding me to Paly and blessing me with the experiences He planned for me. Everything happened for a reason and, in the end, I was blessed with lifelong friends and memories, topped off by a state championship. I could not have asked for more. Next, I want to thank my dad, mom and two brothers for their love, support and help in making me the basketball player I am today. My father raised me playing basketball, mentoring me even to this day. Meanwhile, my mom supported me with hundreds of hours of "team mom" work, and my brothers competed with me everyday and gave me a passion for the game. Furthermore, the Paly basketball team would not be nearly the program it is today without the leadership of Coaches Peter Diepenbrock and Bob Roehl. Although Diepenbrock has instilled a competitive fire and love for the game in his players from day one, I will remember him most for teaching us important life lessons, namely in responsibility, dedication and integrity. Coach Bob has also preached hard work, discipline and teamwork since joining the program this year. Diepenbrock has spent nine years shaping this team into one of the elite programs in the state. His California Coach of the Year award is an understatement. He teaches more than just basketball. Although I ended up with the MVP award, I feel that the plaque should be divided into six pieces and distributed evenly to my senior teammates Steven Brown, Brad Lehman, Cooper Miller, Kheaton Scott and Kevin Trimble. I cannot thank them enough for being true teammates ever since we started playing together during our elementary school years. They picked me up for four years, notably after my season-ending injury last year, and showed me time and time again that no matter how many mistakes I made, I was still part of their basketball family. At the same time, it is equally important to recognize the contributions of Jonny Palmer, Adam Wandell, Connor Baskauskas, Brian Karvelas, Brook Seaman and Josh Bennett. Even though they did not receive the glory and awards, they were as much part of the team as any of the six seniors. Their competitive fire inspired the team in practice, embracing their distinct and essential roles with venerable enthusiasm. Lastly, I am very grateful for the Paly students, staff and community. Paly boys' basketball has not lost at home since March 2003, despite numerous overtime and one-possession games over the last three seasons. The reason is simple:

the fans. The support and the love shown to the basketball team has been truly amazing, and the season would not have ended the same without the fans cheering us on and encouraging us to give our best effort every second. On behalf of the Paly basketball program, I want to thank everyone for supporting our team. Thank you for helping us win our state championship; a championship that we, as a school and community, can share together. It could not have been done without you, and that is not a stretch of my imagination."[57]

Jeremy left Palo Alto High School a champion. His deep-rooted faith, his family values, his work ethic, and his kind spirit remained important examples for the Paly community. Jeremy entered high school at 5-foot-3, with 120 pounds of potential. As he donned his graduation robe and took the stage to receive his diploma, he was now a 6-foot-2 champion. He had grown in mind, body, and spirit, and had transformed into a young man capable of great things. His struggle had never been easy – he faced discrimination, disadvantages, and rejection – but he remained a leader throughout, a humble firebrand who delivered both on and off the court.

Jeremy was now set to embark on the next stage of his life: college. In the months leading up to graduation, however, his college plans were anything but secure.

CHAPTER THREE
Getting Into Harvard

"I wanted to go somewhere the team wanted me. Not somewhere I'd have to go and potentially not have a spot on the team."

—Jeremy Lin, on the college recruitment process

This might be surprising, but Harvard was not Jeremy's dream school. At least not at first. Throughout much of high school, Jeremy had instead dreamed of playing for the UCLA Bruins.[2] The SoCal university was enticing.

For one, Jeremy's brother and role model, Joshua, was a student at the Westwood campus. The university also boasted one of the most successful basketball and academic programs in the nation. It seemed a perfect place for Jeremy – family, basketball, and academics. Here, Jeremy thought he could translate his instincts and intensity into success. He could dominate the court in true blue and gold, as he executed Coach Ben Howland's plays, looking into the crowd at the Pauley Pavilion to see his proud parents and brothers watching his every move. He could be carrying on the legacy of legendary coach John Wooden and his "Pyramid of Success" which taught that excellence in basketball is directly related to excellence in life. (In college, Lin would become a finalist for the national John Wooden Award). What could be better?

And so, the 6-foot-2 Palo Altonian, who loved watching Vince Carter and Tracy McGrady[3], mailed a DVD of his highlights on the court along with his resume (which featured a 4.2 GPA) to UCLA as well as Stanford, Cal State, and all eight Ivy League universities.[4]

But as with every venture in his life, receiving a scholarship to his dream school would pose a challenge for Jeremy. UCLA was a number one seed Division 1 school. In the Central Coast Section of about 125 schools – of which Palo Alto High School belonged – only around three players were drafted to Division I colleges every five years.[5] Moreover, Jeremy was not a nationally known or ranked player at the time. His injury junior year had hurt his chances at national or even statewide notoriety. And by the time the Vikings had returned home as state champions, it was already the winter of senior year, when universities were knee-deep in their recruitment processes.

Race may have played a factor as well. Historically, as in the mid-2000s, there had been hardly any Asian-Americans on Division I men's basketball teams. Coaches and recruiters may have had low expectations – encouraged by unfair stereotypes – for Asian-American high-school players, failing to give them an honest look. Coach Diepenbrock believes that Jeremy's race could have hurt his chances. As Diepenbrock told *The Los Angeles Times*, "If [Lin] was African American or Caucasian, it might have been a different deal."[6]

Lin was also not the player he is today. At the time, a number of universities in the Ivy League, Pac-10, and Patriot Leagues had seen Lin's film footage, but still had doubts about his athleticism and shooting ability.[7]

In any case, Jeremy only heard back from four of the colleges to which he applied. Disappointingly, UCLA "wasn't interested"[8] in the middle Lin child, though the option to walk-on was discussed.[9] The Bruins had instead opted for point guard Mustafa Abdul-Hamid from St. Louis and Russell Westbrook, a shooting guard from Hawthorne, CA. Westbrook – only offered a scholarship once Jordan Farmar chose to go pro – became a powerhouse for the Bruins. Initially, they weren't too remiss about missing out on Lin. However once Lin began to dominate at Harvard, former Bruins assistant Kerry Keating, who had once come to watch a high school game of Lin's, would tell the *San Francisco Chronicle*, "In hindsight, [Lin would] probably be starting for UCLA at point guard."[10] Even in college, his talent was a force of nature. After the peak of "Linsanity," Keating would further explain the situation, in an interview with *The New York Times*. "I said, 'We can't give you a scholarship right away.' I thought he could have played for us. He certainly could have made an impact for us, looking back on it. But at the time, you never really know. It's an inexact science," Keating said.[11] But at the time, it was not in the cards for Jeremy to join his older brother at school.

With UCLA no longer a possibility, Jeremy hoped to attend Stanford. He thought the neighborhood school could be a perfect fit for him. Its location just across the road from Paly was a huge selling point. He could visit home regularly, remain at his church, and watch his little brother play basketball. Besides, Stanford had an incredibly strong basketball program, held membership in the Pac-10, and was a Top 5 nationally ranked university. Maybe Jeremy was meant to hit last-minute 3-pointers or execute power drives in the Maples Pavilion, donning cardinal and white.

In January 2006, Coach Diepenbrock set up a

meeting with Jeremy, Shirley, and Stanford's head coach Trent Johnson. Johnson immediately expressed his interest in the 6-foot-2 point guard. In an interview with *SNY. tv* Diepenbrock recalls Johnson's exact words to Jeremy: "We really want you on the team."[12]

There was a catch, however. Johnson was not offering a scholarship. The Cardinals had already signed Will Paul and twins Brook and Robin Lopez. According to Johnson, Stanford was pursuing two other students but there was only one scholarship remaining. Shirley asked Johnson if neither ended up committing to Stanford, whether Jeremy could get that scholarship. Johnson assured her that he could.[13]

The offer was on the table: Jeremy could walk-on to the team, with the possibility of a scholarship the following year.[14] But in February 2006, both of the players that Stanford was pursuing – Da'Veed Dildy and future Knick teammate Landry Fields – committed to the university. And both players received scholarships.[15] According to reporter Adam Zagoria, "Diepenbrock said Lin and his mother were so turned off by what happened, that when a Stanford assistant tried calling Lin later on to get him to walk-on, he never returned the calls. 'Come on, coach, I can't play for somebody I can't trust,' Diepenbrock recalled Lin saying."[16]

It seemed that Stanford was now out of the question for Lin. So were most of the other universities that
Lin had sent his DVD and resume to. In fact, there were
only two schools that offered Lin a guaranteed place on
their basketball teams – Harvard and Brown. As Lin later
told the *San Francisco Chronicle*, "The Pac-10 schools
wanted me to walk-on. The Ivy League schools, Harvard and Brown, were the two ones that really wanted
me to go there and play for them. I was deciding mainly
between those two conferences…I didn't really want to
walk-on. I wanted to go somewhere the team wanted me.
Not somewhere I'd have to go and potentially not have a
spot on the team."[17]

At first, however, Harvard coaches sought to pass
on the Asian-American. Lin's recruitment hinged on one
man: Bill Holden, an assistant coach at Harvard. Hold-
en first saw Lin at an Amateur Athletic Union tournament in Las Vegas the summer prior to Lin's senior year.
Initially, he was unimpressed. In an interview with *The
New York Times*, Holden expressed his initial disinter-
est. "[Jeremy] didn't really stand out. He was like any
other average high school players we might see. When
I saw his coach, I recommended he go to a Division III
school."[18]

Then, Holden saw Lin play a second time a few

weeks later. It was as if he had stumbled across a completely different player at this A.A.U. tournament. The transformation seemed incredible. Lamar Reddicks, another Harvard assistant, was also watching the game. Jeremy was a tour-de-force that day – a high shooting percentage from beyond the arc, expert communication and passing throughout, Herculean hustle and defensive efforts.

Harvard's head coach, Frank Sullivan, made the trip to the Lin home to sell their now "top recruit."[19] Some time later, Lin accepted the offer. Though the Ivy League does not give out athletic scholarships, Lin was thrilled to play for a team that truly believed in him.

Perhaps the other coaches needed to see Jeremy more than once in order to truly understand the specific dynamism he applies to each game. As Lin told *The New York Times* in 2010, "I just think in order for someone to understand my game, they have to watch me more than once, because I'm not going to do anything that's extra flashy or freakishly athletic."[20] At the end of the day, it was their loss and Harvard's gain.

In the fall of 2006, Lin would be off to the wintry weather of Cambridge, MA, hoping to make his mark on Harvard basketball. Though he may have dreamed of his college years in the warm West Coast sun, he would now be embarking on an exciting journey East. Soon enough, Jeremy would give up palm trees and In-N-Out burgers for pine trees and Bartley's burgers – a Harvard Square favorite. At Harvard, Lin would have the opportunity to inject life into an undervalued basketball program as well as develop and grow as a player.

I've been on the Jeremy Lin bandwagon for a while… I can't take credit for it, but I'm just saying I was there early.

—President Barack Obama, on learning about Lin when the Knicks point guard was still a senior at Harvards

CHAPTER FOUR
The Wonder Years
– Lin's Transformation
at Harvard

It was a rainy Sunday afternoon in Cambridge, MA. The November winds had not yet hinted at the blistering winter that was to befall Harvard's campus in a few short weeks. Nor could the weather forewarn of a 6-foot-2 Asian-American senior who was taking Harvard men's basketball by storm.

On November 15, 2009 the Lavietes Pavilion played host to a crowd of 1,297 for the Harvard Crimson's home opener against William & Mary.[1] The 2,195-seat basketball center boasted a healthy showing that day, but the stands still echoed with emptiness. The arena was far from packed. Perhaps the vacancy was partly a response to the center's mile-long trek from the main reaches of campus. Perhaps the freezing rain was an intimidating alternative to the warm coziness of a Charles River dorm room or library. But more importantly there seemed to exist a deficit in the college's culture of sports fandom.

The most-watched athletic events of Harvard's seasons were the Harvard-Yale football game, the Head of the Charles rowing regatta, and the annual Beanpot ice hockey tournament. Harvard basketball, though popular, was not a must-see, crowd-captivating phenomenon. At least not yet.

Moreover, Harvard prided itself on being well

rounded instead of focused on athletics only. Athletics at the university is as important as the Arts, Sciences and Humanities. Harvard believes that some of the greatest touchdowns are scored in the laboratory; some of the most daring buzzer-beaters achieved on the debate stage. Achievement is prized above all else. Success and growth is the mantra Harvard bestows upon both its undergraduates and graduates, whether on the basketball court or in the classroom.

But it would be foolish to believe that there wasn't something different that cold November day. As Harvard students took to the stands and the game started they soon began to forget about the unfinished essays awaiting them. For now a feeling was beginning to take hold. It was not yet a mania - "Linsanity" would not become a full-blown pandemic until two and half years later. For now, it was simply a feeling. A tickle. An instinct. A reaction. There was something about the senior co-captain from Palo Alto.

Most of the fans were there to see Jeremy, having become enchanted by his talents the previous season. There were even a few signs boasting Lin's number – number 4. The Leverett House contingent – from Lin's upperclassmen dorm – was in full force. Even new spectators were attending to finally see the Palo Alto High alumnus in action. Still, some in the crowd did not know who Jeremy was. But as soon as the whistle blew and the clock started, they would find out. It was to be the start of another tremendous season for Jeremy. And his reputation was about to grow.

The game kicked off with a current of aggressive defense that was soon challenged by muted offensive plays.[2] Harvard had a habit of running down the shot clock without mounting offensive drives.[3] The lead fluctuated throughout the game as the score remained tremendously close each quarter.

By the end of the fourth quarter the Tribe and the Crimson were tied, taking the game into the first five-minute overtime. Neither team was able to run away with a significant lead for much of the first two overtimes, taking the contest into a third.[4] Teammates Keith Wright, Oliver McNally, and Pat Magnarelli helped Lin reduce the deficit throughout post-regulation time. But with just four seconds to go, Tribe guard Sean McCurdy nailed a lay-up pushing the visitors into the lead, 85-84.

With just moments left, Lin received the inbound pass and headed for the basket. He was met at the half-court line, but pushed forward a few steps before being knocked to the ground by the Tribe defender. On his way down, with one second remaining, Lin threw up the shot.

The ball soared through the air. The tension in the crowd was palpable. All eyes locked on Lin.

* * *

In September 2006, a tall, lanky, Asian-American freshman walked through the famed Harvard Yard on his way to class. He passed a throng of Chinese tourists armed with Canons and Kodaks relatively unnoticed. Lin was on his way to shop or test out an introductory economics class called "Economics 10" at Sanders Theater, the largest lecture hall on Harvard's campus. It was one of the most popular classes on campus, a requirement for all Economics majors. Lin was no exception.

Jeremy was just another freshman; He lived in Harvard Yard; he wore his DHAS (Department of Harvard Athletics) sweatpants around campus – traditional jock attire; and he ate his meals at Annenberg Hall with the other freshmen. Still, his maturity was apparent. He would stay in nights to study or rest up for the following day's practice, at times forgoing Saturday night parties or weekday hang-out sessions. He came to Harvard for a reason, and he would do everything to support his success. At the time, he was no one special. He was just a kid who was wildly intelligent and had tremendous potential on the basketball court. He came to Harvard as a top recruit with a lot to learn. During the beginning of his first year on the squad, under Coach Frank Sullivan's leadership, his performances were uneventful.[5]

In an interview with *GQ*, fellow freshman recruit Alek Blankenau recalled Lin's initial shortcomings. "He was by far the weakest person on the team," Blankenau remembers.[6] Assistant coach Reddick confirms those sentiments, revealing that he and others "considered Lin the weakest player on the team."[7]

But for Lin, weaknesses and shortcomings proved to be excellent motivation. Jeremy immediately worked toward becoming more dominant on the court, honing his skills and reverting to the basics.

Slowly, Lin began to gain traction. Though he didn't start, Lin played in all twenty-eight games held during the 2006-2007 season, averaging just under 19 minutes a game.[8] He shot .818 from the free throw line, .415 from the field, and .281 from beyond the arc, averaging 4.8 points and 1.8 assists per game.[9] Lin showed "court awareness" and a "knowledge of off-ball defense," even hitting the game-winning basket against the University of New Hampshire on November 29 – something that would be come a trend in the coming years.[10] He had 10 points, four assists and three steals in the 18 minutes he played against Yale on January 26, and another 9 points and 3 assists in the 14 minutes he played against Cornell in March. The Crimson won ythat game 85-79.[11] Lin was showing promise, but lacked consistency. His instincts were impressive, but his performance needed some fine-tuning.

It seems a common theme throughout Jeremy's life that early struggle is simply a hurdle on the road to the wild success that awaits him. For Jeremy, it is all in the timing. Sophomore year would follow the same trajectory. The 2007-2008 season brought a changing of the guard and with it a unique opportunity for Jeremy.

Head Coach Frank Sullivan was fired after the Crimson went 12-16 the previous season and was replaced by Tommy Amaker, a former All-American point guard who played for the legendary Mike Krzyzweski and the Duke Blue Devils.[12] The two clicked instantly – Amaker was taken by the devout sophomore and his work ethic, while the knowledge the former point guard had to offer inspired Lin. It was a "bromance" of sorts. They were in total sync with each other. One of the main values they shared was self-improvement.

Will Wade, an assistant for Harvard during Lin's sophomore and junior years, confirms that Amaker helped mold Lin for future success.[13] "Jeremy was a very, very driven kid. A kid who had a lot of layers to him. But what really spurred his growth was that coach Amaker took a vested interest in his development. Coach Amaker saw things in Jeremy that he probably didn't see in himself," Wade said in an interview with the NBA's Chris Dortch .[14]

Lin was still a novice, and Amaker's guidance seemed finally to chart a concrete path to success. As Wade recalls, "[Lin] was a tremendous worker. He was always wanting to learn, always asking questions. Sometimes, he would get frustrated with himself because he wasn't progressing at the rate he wanted to progress. For him, it was great having Coach Amaker mentor and guide him."[15]

Amaker and Lin's close relationship greatly influenced the point guard. During his sophomore season, Lin was the only player to start in all 30 games, averaging 12.6 points per game, a .448 shooting percentage and earning 107 assists.[16] He racked up 58 steals, the most in the Ivy League, and ranked among the league's leaders in all other categories.[17] He had a season high of 21 points against the University of Pennsylvania in February and was awarded Player of the Week on February 25, 2008.[18]

The season was a hallmark for Lin. He received the

team's Raymond P. Lavietes '36 Most Valuable Player Award and was named to the All-Ivy League Second Team.[19] It was an important year for Lin, a time when he needed to shine. In true Lin style, he delivered and then some. It was the first ripple in the start of a successful career with the Crimson, and a telling foreword to his apprenticeship with Amaker.

Equally as important, in March of 2008 Lin earned a place on the Ivy Honor Roll for academic achievement.[20] His prowess on the court was matched by his diligence in the classroom. Ever a gifted student, Lin channeled his work ethic to all other aspects of his life, including his schoolwork. Economics was to be Lin's academic focus, though religion was perhaps his true calling.

While at Harvard, Lin was a leader in the Harvard-Radcliffe Asian-American Christian Fellowship.[21] His junior and senior years Lin served as a co-leader for a Bible study group on campus.[22] He also worked with the InterVarsity Christian Fellowship/USA, "a Christian student organization that focuses on small-group Bible studies."[23] Jeremy's devout faith even inspired some non-religious teammates to take part on the weekly meetings.[24] As *The Harvard Crimson* reported, on Saturdays, Lin "would text [his friends], reminding them to go to bed early so they could get their rest before waking up for church."[25] On Sundays, Lin "rounded up the others to head over to church together."[26] There was no pomp and circumstance with Jeremy. He led by example and he followed through. His devout nature – his commitment to God, to his family, to his studies and to basketball – was an example to all who knew him.

But college ball also presented hardships for an Asian-American student. Players and fans of opposing teams would make incendiary remarks about Jeremy's ethnicity. As Lin shot free throws, one student yelled "Won-ton soup."[27] But the taunts, which had started years ago, no longer seemed to phase Jeremy. As he told *ESPN*, "I do get tired of it; I just want to play. But I've also come to accept it and embrace it. If I help other kids, then it's worth it."[28]

By junior year, talk of Jeremy's standout sopho-more season started to make the rounds of Harvard's campus. It failed to incite a crazed basketball movement, but the small collection of Crimson basketball devotees began to convince the less faithful to come out for games and take stock in the kid they knew from Economics sec-tion or the Leverett dining hall. And so, Jeremy started the season with confidence. He was now an upperclass-man and newly minted co-captain of the team. The title meant a lot to Jeremy, simply because it symbolized the high esteem and respect his teammates shared for him. Slowly but surely a new group of faces appeared in Lavietes Pavilion. They were there to watch the Crimson play, but they were also there to see Jeremy.

On Wednesday, January 7, 2009, a single game would change everything. The Crimson took on No. 17 Boston College, which was enjoying a 10-game winning streak and a recent upset victory over then No. 1 North Carolina.[29] The game, held at BC's Conte Forum, was supposed to be an easy victory for the Eagles. It would turn out to be anything but.

Led by Jeremy, the Crimson were unstoppable, posting up impressive percentages from both inside and outside the arc, executing tight defense, and demonstrating hustle. By the game's end, the Crimson had upset Boston College 82-70. Lin scored a game-high 27 points, going 11 of 16 from the floor, with 6 steals, 2 blocks, 3 rebounds, and 8 assists.[30] *The Harvard Crimson* called it "the game of [Lin's] career,"[31] while Amaker sung his praises, telling the school paper "'I can't give enough credit to Jeremy and the rest of our kids for the effort they put forth.'"[32]

News of the game – and Lin's performance – reached national outlets. Newspapers, magazines, and television programs were reporting on Harvard's win and the Asian-American point guard who led them to victory. Highlights of the game even appeared on *ESPN's SportsCenter*. The nation had finally been introduced to Jeremy Lin.

Lin's success continued throughout the season. According to his Harvard Athletics profile, he was "the only player to rank nationally among the top 10 players in his conference in every statistical category."[33] He ranked third in scoring at 17.8 points per game, second in assists at 4.3 per game, first in steals at 68 for the season and 2.4 per game, sixth in field goal percentage at .502, seventh in 3-point percentage at .400, eighth in free throw percentage at .744, first in free throw attempts with 168 and made free-throws with 125, ninth in rebounding at 5.5 per game, and tenth in blocked shots with 18.[34]

The achievements seemed endless as he became a part of the NABC All-District 1 First Team, scored an invite to the All-Ivy League First Team, and was featured in a USA Today piece on February 23 as one of the "top five players or teams that [USA Today] wished had more television exposure."[35]

During Lin's junior season, he also scored his 1,000[th] point, a feat accomplished by just six other athletes in Harvard's history.[36] On top of all of that, Jeremy was "named to Ivy League Honor Roll in 13 of the 15 weekly reports [for the season], earning player of the week honors twice."[37]

The accolades and triumphs were undoubtedly the result of painstaking hard work and dedication. Will Wade was stunned by the transformation. "He wasn't a great shooter [when he first came to Harvard]. He was pretty good in the mid range, but he didn't have range to 3. People would back off and play him as a driver, so he'd force shots and not get as many clean looks. Jeremy worked hard on expanding his range. That made his pull-up jumper almost deadly, and when he was able to be a consistent threat from 3, it opened up the whole floor for him," Wade acknowledged.[38] "That's why, in Jeremy's junior year, it was his team. Coach Amaker basically gave him the keys to the bus and said, 'Let's go.'"[39] But Jeremy's greatest feats were to come the following season, as the senior on the team.

* * *

As the winter returned in late 2009, so too did Jeremy's exploits on the court. Senior year was a new ballgame for Lin. He was no longer an unknown, an underdog, a simply solid player. He was enjoying a wave of rock-star status throughout campus. Professors recognized him immediately among seas of students during large lecture classes. The dining hall staff would stop him on the street and wish him luck for the following day's game. Even the librarians abandoned their posts to strike up a conversation with Lin. Harvard students, faculty, alumni, and staff were excited by him, by Coach Amaker's magic touch, and by the success of the entire men's basketball team the season prior. Now, Lin was the man to watch.

It was a rainy November day during the Crimson's home opener that year, Lin's final year on the Harvard squad. William and Mary had forced the Crimson into a third overtime.[40] A lasting excitement permeated the stands, feet stomping, hands clapping, eyes wide open. It seemed everyone was thinking the same thought: this is not typical Harvard basketball. The third overtime was a closely choreographed battle of endurance and technique. The Crimson and the Tribe kept the game neck-and-neck responding to lay-ups with jump shots, and effecting spirited defense.

Down by one with four seconds left, Lin took the inbound pass, marched to half-court and with seconds on the clock took a shot he'd never taken before.[41] All eyes locked on Lin. Deafening silence overpowered the arena. The buzzer sounded. And then it hit. The 30-foot shot effortlessly swished. The Crimson took home an 87-85 win over William & Mary.

The Harvard Crimson, the college's official daily newspaper, recalled the scene: "Trailed by a throng of ecstatic teammates, co-captain Jeremy Lin leapt and ran up the wall at the near end of Lavietes Pavilion. It was an appropriate celebration for Harvard's superhero, who had just come up huge in the clutch yet again."[42] Jeremy found divinity in his shot. "'That was a prayer – God just guided it into the hoop, that's the best way I can describe it,'" Lin said.[43] If it hadn't been convinced before, the entire campus was now officially won over by the college superstar.

Lin's senior year saw him take his game to new heights. The quality of the team had improved as a whole, so Lin's stats were somewhat lower than his stats a year earlier. Similarly, Lin was now on every team's radar, and was often double-teamed by opponents. But the subtle hints of "Linsanity" were turning into a full-fledged pandemic. On December 6, 2009, the Crimson took on the No. 13-seed University of Connecticut. It was to be yet another Lin-centric game that would have people talking for a long time.

From the outset the Crimson were the clear underdogs, and the UConn Huskies took full advantage in the first half. But under Lin's leadership, the Crimson mounted an impressive comeback in the second.[44] Lin was a powerhouse throughout – his steals, jump shots, and lay-ups sought to create momentum for Harvard. Ultimately, UConn would outplay the Crimson, fending off a major upset, with a final score of 79-73.[45]

Regardless of the 6-point loss, the Lin phenomenon had shown itself once again. Lin scored 30 points throughout the game, and logged 3 steals, 3 assists, 9 rebounds and 2 blocks.[46] His strategy and athleticism was almost intoxicating in the Storrs, Connecticut gymnasium. "For some folks who haven't seen [Lin] play, you're probably wowed by some of the things he can do – we are," Coach Amaker told *The Harvard Crimson*.[47] Lin's performance captivated the hearts and minds of Crimson fans and college basketball fans everywhere. The Asian-American point guard's domination once again made national news. Even UConn coach Jim Calhoun was thoroughly impressed by Lin, stating, "He's one of the better kids, including Big East guards, who have come in here in quite some time."[48]

But Jeremy was just being Jeremy. He continued a stellar season scoring 25 points against Boston College, (upsetting them for a second straight year), 19 points against Dartmouth, and 24 points in the second Cornell game of the season.[49]

That year, Lin traveled ground previously untouched in the Ivy League. He became the first player in Ivy League history to record 1,450 points, 450 rebounds, 400 assists and 200 steals.[50] He ranks first in games played at the school, fifth in points, fifth in assists, and second in steals.[51] He scored an average of 16.4 points per game, and earned 131 assists.[52] He was named one of the country's 12 most versatile players by ESPN, a member of the 2010 Lou Henson All-American team, one of 11 finalists for the Bob Cousy Award (which goes to the nation's top point guard), one of 20 finalists for the John R. Wooden Award (which goes to the national player of the year) He was named to the Ivy Honor Roll time and again.[53]

Lin had made his mark at one of the world's foremost institutions and started to gain traction on the national stage. As Amaker told *The Harvard Crimson*, "[Jeremy is] the best [basketball] player to ever play at Harvard. Period."[54] But he was not finished. He had changed the face of Harvard basketball forever, and was now looking for a career in the big leagues. He graduated in May 2010 with a degree in Economics and a 3.1 GPA.[55] Lin's path to NBA superstardom would be rocky, but he was used to such hardship. In fact, he thrived in those situations.

As his college career drew to a close, one thing Lin wouldn't miss about Harvard were the bitter winter winds. Little did he know that in a few short years, he would be battling the same winter chill in a town four hours south of Boston – New York City.

CHAPTER FIVE
A Bumpy Road to
the NBA

I n May of 2010, Jeremy's classmates gathered in a sea of black robes in Tercentenary Theater. The crowd of proud students and families clamored to hear President Drew Faust bestow Harvard degrees upon the Class of 2010.

The Lins, however, were notably absent. Jeremy was instead more than 3,000 miles away, in Los Angeles, working out for the Lakers in pre-draft trials.[1] On a trip back to Cambridge, Lin finally picked up his diploma. As he told *The Boston Herald*, "I just went to the registrar's office and picked it up. It was in an envelope. Not much of a celebration. I showed both my IDs and picked it up and headed on my way... It's kind of crazy – four years and I'm finally able to get a piece of paper that officialized [sic] everything."[2]

But a hopeful journey to the big leagues started on a disappointing note for the Harvard graduate. As *The New York Times* reported, "eight teams invited [Lin] to pre-draft workouts, then he was overlooked through 2 rounds and 60 players chosen."[3]

It was not that Lin wasn't talented; it was more that his talents didn't translate to the workouts, which were composed differently than regulation games. As Lin explained to the *Times*, "[The workouts are] skill work, some shooting, and they're one on one or two on two or three on three, and that's not where I excel. I've never played basketball like that."[4]

That fall, Jeremy failed to be picked in the 2010 NBA Draft. It was a crushing moment for an individual who had come so far, since his days as a 5-foot-3, 120-pound freshman at Palo Alto High School. After all, this seemed to be the "Year of Jeremy." His exploits were written up by *Sports Illustrated*, *ESPN*, even *TIME Magazine*. But attention and record-breaking Ivy League play didn't necessarily translate into opportunity.

Well, there was one opportunity on the table. An invitation came in the form of a position on the Dallas Mavericks' summer-league team. Jeremy's senior year triumph at Harvard had left an impression on General Manager Donnie Nelson and the Mavs scouts.[5] Lin took what he could get.

Lin headed to Las Vegas. He was not used to "Sin City," his own values very different from the vice and extravagance that filled the Nevada metropolis. But Lin ignored the casinos and the variety shows, instead focusing on what he came there to do.

In his first five games, Lin was consistent, though not extraordinary. He kept up with the other players, at times taking advantage of his strengths, but he did not yet make a splash. The sixth and final game, however, changed everything. Up against the No. 1 NBA draft choice John Wall, Lin turned it on. *The New York Times* recreated the moment:

> "In the fourth quarter, Lin forced a jump ball with Wall, made a steal, tore a rebound from a 7-footer, hit a 3-pointer and made a rousing spin move that drew a charging call, dredging boos from the crowd. In the days that followed, the phones rang."[6]

News of the showdown with Wall made the rounds in Las Vegas. The Mavs immediately made an offer – a one-year guaranteed contract with the understanding that Lin would develop with the Texas Legends, Dallas' D-League affiliate.[7]

The offer was certainly not a golden ticket any-where. But if it had been the only possible opportunity, it was likely that Jeremy would have taken it. After all, here was a young man who failed to garner a scholarship from his dream schools. Instead, he took a position at a university with a less-than-stellar basketball program, transforming himself, his team, and even the program into a force to be reckoned with.

Luckily for Jeremy, though, there were other offers on the table – including an offer from the Los Angeles Lakers[8]. But one offer in particular hit a lot closer to home. The Golden State Warriors offered Jeremy a two-year deal with more guarantees.[9] It would be his first chance, since high school, to play for the home team. Luck seemed to be on Jeremy's side.

Jeremy accepted the offer with the Warriors. "I just remember saying, 'I can't believe this!'" Lin told *The New York Times*. "I was yelling. I was fist pumping. I was screaming. I can't remember all that I said, but if you were anywhere near my house, you probably would have heard me."[10]

Warriors general manager Larry Riley was thrilled about the addition. As he told the *Star-Telegram*, "[Lin's] a player who had a good feel for the game. He seemed to understand what it was all about. He had the uncanny ability to get into the middle from time to time. He's a guy who stood out because he was always in the right place at the right time."[11] Still, as with any new player, there were concerns. "He couldn't shoot," Riley admitted. "We wondered if he could defend quick point guards. My take on it was if he gets better, he could probably be a backup point guard in the league."[12]

What happened in Vegas did not stay in Vegas. In fact, as soon as Jeremy's deal became official, he became the toast of the town and the talk of the nation. News outlets everywhere were clamoring for an interview with the NBA star – the fourth ever Asian-American to play in the NBA (and the first of Taiwanese or Chinese descent).[13]

Journalists hounded the Warriors Press Office, chased after Jeremy during games, and even pursued Gie-Ming and Shirley at home. After all, the news of the deal was a revelation for the Bay area. Many had been tracking Jeremy's journey since the beginning of his career – first as a phenomenon at Paly, then as a phenomenon at Harvard. For the Asian-American community at home and throughout the nation, Jeremy's ascension into the NBA was particularly meaningful.

Even Jeremy understood the importance of his journey and the effect it might have on those in his community. As he told *Sports Illustrated*, "Just my whole story is so unique. Not only Asian-American, I'm from Harvard, from the Bay Area, I was virtually unknown coming into the draft scene. Not once – never – was I on anybody's draft board coming in. Everyone just kind of removed me from the picture once the season ended. My emergence was so sudden," Lin said.[14]

As the Warriors started the season, it was clear the fans were coming to see a particular 6-foot-2 un-drafted rookie. At the Oracle Center fans went wild any time Lin was mentioned or subbed-in – or even any time he was not. The Warrior-faithful would chant Jeremy's name throughout regulation time, and collectively call for coach Keith Smart to get Lin in the game.[15]

But the fans' love for Lin was not met with the same level of performance that Lin had demonstrated so often throughout high school and college. The NBA was the "big leagues," and it proved to be a more difficult stomping ground.

By December 2010, the Warriors had made the decision to transfer Lin to their Development League affiliate-team, the Reno Bighorns. Lin had appeared in 17 games so far, but only averaged 1.9 points and 8.5 minutes.[16] Although he made an impressive showing in November against the Lakers, with a then-career high 13 points, he failed to make the impact the Warriors had hoped for. Coaches felt that Lin needed "game repetition" in order to solidify the skills he had been working on.[17]

Lin was sent to the D-League on three occasions. Each visit carried a specific purpose. In his first D-League tour he worked on "developing his pick-and-roll game."[18] On his second, he focused on "how to take a blow on the drive and still get off the shot" and "how to read and attack defensive double-teams."[19] His third tour called for "[smoothing] out his jumper and [becoming] more confident in his 3-point shot."[20]

For anyone else, a visit to the D-League would have felt like a demotion. For Lin, it was an opportunity to improve. After each visit, Lin returned to the Warriors' bench, averaging 2.6 points by the end of the season. Lin was an inexpensive wildcard who had received the training that he needed and deserved. The Warriors were guardedly hopeful for his sophomore debut next season.

The off-season presented a new realm of possibility for Lin. It would be his time to transform yet again. His experiences at training in the previous season had encouraged him to reinvent his body and his game. His efforts coincided with the 2011 NBA lockout – which lasted from July to December 2011 – giving Lin ample time for a true metamorphosis.

Over the next few months, Lin would enlist the help of three superstars – Doc Scheppler, Phil Wagner, and E.J. Costello.[21] Lin had known Scheppler since middle school. In fact, Scheppler had once coached Peter Diepenbrock, Lin's high school coach and mentor.[22] The Pinewood High School girls basketball coach sought to help Lin improve his shooting ability. Lin suffered from two fundamental flaws – "he brought the ball too far behind his head" and "he started his shooting motion too late."[23]

Scheppler worked on increasing stability and a quicker release in Lin's shot.[24] He even introduced a game called "Beating the Ghost" to develop Jeremy's 3-point abilities. The premise of the game was that Jeremy would stand at the three-point line and take shots. For every basket he scored he earned 1 point. For each basket he missed, the invisible "Ghost" earned 3 points. If the "Ghost" beat Jeremy to 21, it was game over.[25]

Jeremy wouldn't quit until he beat the "Ghost" which often took numerous attempts. The *Mercury News* calculates that Jeremy must have taken "500 to 600 shots over the course of 1 ½ hours, three to four times a week" to perfect his shot.[26] Scheppler was impressed with Lin's devotion and capacity to improve. As he told the paper, "That's the lesson here: if you don't like the way things are going for you in a sport, don't cry about it. Don't whine to this coach. Do something about it."[27]

His two trainers – Phil Wagner at Sparta Performance Science facility and E.J. Costello at the local 24 Hour Fitness – worked tirelessly to help Lin increase his strength and agility. Weeks of strength training resulted in an additional 15 pounds of muscle, increasing his weight to 212 pounds, and an increase of 3.5 inches in his vertical leap.[28] In an interview with *The New York Times*, Wagner explained Lin's results: "Before, he was a motorcycle: he was maneuverable, but very off-balance," Wagner said. "Now he's like a Porsche: he's fast, but he's stable."[29]

There was a new fire in Lin. He was now a different player – stronger, faster, more accurate. The lockout had been a blessing in disguise for the Harvard alum because it gave him ample time to develop. Jeremy's journey to the NBA had been an epic struggle, from undrafted to fan-favorite, from previous inconsistency to a newfound stability. As always, Lin became the player he needed to become under the given circumstances.

The stakes were now raised and Jeremy believed that over the course of the past few months he had risen to challenge and developed into a player who was now ready for excellence on the court. He was excited to show his coaches and teammates his transformation.

Unfortunately, he would never get that chance. At least not as a Warrior.

CHAPTER SIX
From the End of
the Bench

On December 8, 2011 the NBA lockout was officially over, and pre-season had begun. On December 9, during the first day of Warriors training camp, Lin was cut from the team. His waiver was a financial move to gain capital for a new free agent who Golden State felt might have a greater impact on the team.[1]

It was a frustrating setback for the hometown hero and for his family, friends, and fans. No longer would the Paly alum be able to represent the place that meant most to him. The suddenness of the release did nothing to soften the blow.

But the unexpected momentum of NBA business quickly rebounded for the middle Lin child. Three days later on December 12, the Houston Rockets claimed Lin off waivers from the Warriors.[2]

The prospect of playing for the Rockets was exciting. It had been the franchise of two of the greatest NBA players of all time: Moses Malone and Hakeem Olajuwon. It was not so long ago that Gie-Ming Lin had watched and recorded all of those hours of Malone's games – the hook shots, the drives, the three-pointers – and taught his son in that image of greatness. It was also the former team of Yao Ming, one of Lin's mentors, who made an indelible mark on the NBA.

With so many guards already on the team, Lin questioned how long he would really have on the team. "At the time, I was thinking if this doesn't work out, I maybe needed to take a break from basketball," Lin told the *Mercury News*. "I put in four months of training. I felt like I worked harder than anyone else. And now I was fighting for a chance to practice. I was questioning everything."[3]

Unfortunately, Lin would not call the Toyota Center home for long. After two pre-season games, and a total of 7 minutes, 51 seconds of playing time, Lin was waived.[4] It happened on Christmas Eve. As with Golden State, the Rockets were looking to use that money to bring in a bigger name.[5] It was all business. Later, after the reign of "Linsanity," Houston's general manager Daryl Morey took to his Twitter account to air his regrets. "We should have kept [Jeremy Lin]. Did not know he was that good," Morey wrote.[6]

The volatility of the business was extremely difficult for Lin, who just wanted to play ball. One of his closest friends from his days at Harvard, Kai-Cheng Ho, saw Lin shortly after the waiver. "He was very discouraged," Ho told *The Harvard Crimson*. "Everyone thinks NBA life is glamorous, but they don't understand how challenging it is. Everyone was telling him what to do and what not to do."[7]

In each of the chapters of Jeremy's life there had been substantial adversity. Sometimes it was minor, other times it seemed undefeatable. But time and again, Jeremy persevered – through faith and family – and overcame whatever obstacle kept him from his dream.

As former roommate Eric Lee said about the situation, "When times are tough, it just made [Jeremy] work that much harder. It was a roller coaster ride. He was always plugging away, trying to outwork the next guy, trying to better himself."[8] In fact, many of the miraculous moments in Lin's life came after a period of initial struggle. This time would be no different.

Three days after getting waived, on December 27, the Knicks claimed Lin off waivers to lend support for injured rookie guard Iman Shumpert. Lin was an unknown factor to the Knicks. As coach Mike D'Antoni told *The New York Times*, "We didn't know if he could defend well enough. We didn't know whether he could finish well enough. And we didn't know if he could shoot outside well enough. We did like his playmaking ability. We liked his ability to get in the paint. We liked that he was unselfish. We liked that he was smart. We liked that he had all the intangibles of being a point guard."[9] But Lin still had a lot to prove.

The Knicks coaching staff quickly noticed the work Lin had accomplished over the prior few months. He was a more athletic, substantial player than the young man they had seen in 2010. But this was a new team, and Lin felt he had to prove himself once more. Lin found refuge in his work ethic. Lin once again committed his all to every training session. *The New York Times* recalled his habits at the time:

"[Lin] was the first to arrive every day, and the last to leave. He sought and devoured game tapes. When he requested his own clips, Lin asked to see his turnovers and missed jumpers, not his assists. In side sessions with the assistant Kenny Atkinson, Lin kept working on his jump shot and his decision making in pick-and-roll situations. The coaches instantly recognized his ability to blow past defenders, but without much regard for what he would do once he beat them. So they worked on footwork, judgment ad subtle movements to freeze a defender. The work continued, quietly and without much notice, for five weeks..."[10]

Jeremy had once again adapted to the situation he found himself in. He was no longer the same player that

Paly fans had lauded, nor the same player that Harvard swooned over, nor even the same player that brought the Golden State faithful to their knees. No, this was, once again, a new and improved Jeremy. This was the newest version of Jeremy Lin the NBA star. He was older, taller, heavier, abler, more skilled, and more athletic. But all of these changes stemmed from the same work ethic, the same faith, and the same values that Gie-Ming and Shirley had taught their son over twenty years ago. Jeremy was always Jeremy. But Jeremy was always someone new. He sought perfection in his sport, and so yet again, he worked with the trainers to do everything possible to become the best Knicks player he could be.

During these five weeks, Lin saw little playing time. He first hit the court on December 28, the day after being claimed by the Knicks. It was an away game for the Knicks, but a true home game for Jeremy. The Knicks were playing his former team, the Golden State Warriors. Just a few years had changed so much. Now, Lin had swapped the gold and blue for orange and blue. It wasn't by choice, of course.

The crowd gave Lin a warm welcome. The third-string point guard garnered just a few minutes of playing time, but missed the only shot he took – a 19-footer.[11] Needless to say, the homecoming was uneventful.

In mid-January, a few days after Lin once again saw playing time against the Oklahoma City Thunder, the Knicks decided to send Jeremy – along with rookie center Jerome Jordan – to their Development League affiliate team, the Erie BayHawks.[12]

Lin had only scored 5 points and executed 2 assists throughout the season so far.[13] Mike D'Antoni explained to reporter Adam Zagoria that it was simply a way to offer more playing time to Lin and Jordan. "They'll be back pretty soon," D'Antoni said. "There's not enough practices. They were just sitting there. We do want them to play and be in game condition in case you need them. This is the perfect time to do it now."[14]

On January 20, the Erie Bayhawks – replete with new teammate Jeremy Lin – faced-off against the Maine Red Claws in Portland, Maine. Portland was a far cry from New York, the nation's biggest city, and the D-League game must have seemed a world away from the Garden, where the Knicks were tanking against the Milwaukee Bucks (a game that ended 100-86). But in the large New England city, Lin was having the game of the season.

It had the essence of his high school championship against Mater Dei, the aura of the Harvard upset against Boston College. By the time the night was over, Lin had scored a triple-double – hitting double digits in points, rebounds and assists. In 44 minutes Lin scored 28 points, had 12 assists, and 11 rebounds.[15]

News from Portland hit New York City, where the Knicks were still reeling from a devastating loss. Just days later, on January 23, D'Antoni booked Lin a flight back to New York.[16] Lin was encouraged by the trip to Erie. He viewed it as another opportunity to gain meaningful playing time and develop as a player, much like during his three assignments with the Reno Big Horns. He would later tell Zagoria that the trip was important. "It definitely helped me because they run the same system in Erie and I think that's proper development, I guess," Lin said. "It helped me a lot and Jerome a lot, too, actually, just learning to work together, work the pick and roll, understand the chemistry, the flow, the pace."[17]

Lin sought to make good on his promising run in Portland. He was starting to click with the Knicks' rhythm. In fact, Lin's old coach, Tommy Amaker, felt that Lin was a perfect fit for D'Antoni's offensive system.[18] "I think the style of play, the fit there, is ideal for Jeremy," Amaker told *New England Sports Network*. "The spacing the floor, the pick-and-roll, I think it's ideally suited to who he is."[19]

Jeremy was ready to get back on the court, this

time in his blue and orange. He played for 20 minutes against the Rockets on January 28 and 6 minutes against Detroit on the 31st. The little playing time didn't allow for much in the way of points or rebounds, steals or assists, though Jeremy did manage 6 assists in the Houston game and 4 against Detroit.[20]

For most of regulation time, however, Jeremy took his spot at the end of the bench. On February 3, the Knicks gave up a lead to the Boston Celtics in the fourth quarter. In "desperation," D'Antoni called Jeremy from the end of the bench in place of Guard Toney Douglas. It wasn't significant playing time – just 7 minutes – but it seemed to ignite a spark.[21] When asked what he was hoping to accomplish in playing Lin, D'Antoni told *AOL Sports*, "Just anything. Just trying to find some kind of rhyme or reason to things. Haven't quite found it yet."[22]

The following night the Knicks played the New Jersey Nets at the Garden. The Knicks were off to a poor start. With 3:34 left to go in the first quarter, Iman Shumpert had missed three shots, thrown a bad pass, and committed two fouls. D'Antoni was desperately looking to shake things up on the court. He reconfigured the lineup in his mind. Then, almost out of nowhere, he scanned the bench. It took him the length of the row to find where he was going.

There, at the end of the bench, Coach D'Antoni's eyes locked on Jeremy. With 3:34 left to in the first quarter, Jeremy Lin entered the game for Shumpert. It was to be a memorable night.

CHAPTER SEVEN
Linsanity

February 4, 2012 – New York Knicks vs.
New Jersey Nets

Everything changed on February 4, 2012. Little did Coach D'Antoni know, when he looked to the end of the bench and saw a 6-foot-2, 212 pound, Harvard Economics degree holding, "Beat the Ghost" acing, high school state championship winning Asian-American, that in just a few short days this 23-year-old would become a worldwide phenomenon.

All D'Antoni knew at that moment was that the Knicks needed to try something new. D'Antoni sent Lin into the game with just over three minutes remaining in the first quarter against the New Jersey Nets.

His first quarter play was pretty standard, but in the second quarter he started to find his groove. Lin hit a team high of 6 points with 3 assists, hustling to get back quickly to deliver strong defense against All-Star Deron Williams. He executed tight pick-and-rolls and expertly paced the flow of the ball. The continued dynamism and another 7 points in the third quarter kept the Nets within a 2-point deficit. But it was the fourth quarter where Lin finally unleashed – for the world to see – all that he had been training for more than 10 years.

Each stage of Lin's transformation as a player was

available that night – the jump shots he learned from Diepenbrock, the power drives he picked up from Amaker, and the 3-pointers he perfected with Scheppler. Lin made an early 19-foot jumper in the quarter, followed by an assist to Jared Jeffries and another 14-foot shot with eight minutes to go, giving the Knicks another 3 points. In the next seven minutes, Jeremy would score 8 more points, widening the Knicks lead to a healthy 9 points, and carrying them into the final seconds of the game for a 99-92 win.[1]

Madison Square Garden erupted. Pearl Jam's "Jeremy" blasted over the PA system.[2] Jeremy Lin – untested as a Knicks asset – scored a career high of 25 points, with 5 rebounds, 7 assists, and 2 steals. He controlled the court with cool, expert instinct and injected new life into a Knicks squad that desperately needed it. The performance was nothing short of miraculous. *The New York Times* called it a "performance born of necessity."[3] Coach D'Antoni hailed Lin's performance as "something we sorely needed," praising Lin for his "point-guard mentality."[4] Amid a deafening cheer from Knicks fans, Lin went to the locker room where he was promptly hounded by the media.

The superstar performance soon became national news. Video recaps of the game popped up on *SportsCen-*

ter, YouTube, even nightly news programs. The Harvard kid with the unique pedigree had quickly become an overnight sensation. But the true test would be whether this could last. Was it a fluke or the beginning of something real?

February 6, 2012 - New York Knicks v. Utah Jazz

Two nights later, the Knicks returned to the Garden to take on the Utah Jazz. Two Knicks stars – Amare Stoudemire and Carmelo Anthony – were notably absent. The prospects of beating the Jazz looked dim without the two leaders.

But the Knicks were still reeling from the effects of the sensation from Palo Alto. Lin's 25-point game two nights earlier had caused celebration throughout New York.

Coach D'Antoni started Lin, with the hope that the point guard would be able to repeat the previous game's triumph. But Jeremy didn't just repeat it. He improved on it. He picked up his driving game and continued a slew of pick-and-rolls. Capitalizing on the momentum, the rest of the Knicks team kept pace with Lin, moving the ball around and using their strengths and position to cause real damage.

Up 51-38 at the half, the Knicks continued the pace of their lead, with Jeremy outmaneuvering Jazz defense. By the end of the game Jeremy had amassed 28 points – a new career high – going 10-17 from the field, with 8 assists, 2 rebounds, and 2 steals. Once again, Lin lit up the New Yorkers in the crowd. Now, signs with "#17" and "I love you Jeremy" adorned Madison Square Garden. Lin was on a roll.

February 8, 2012 - New York Knicks v. Washington Wizards

D'Antoni's guess-and-check method had finally paid off. He had discovered the point guard who could expertly lead the team. As D'Antoni told *ESPN*, "It's fun, you can actually draw a play up and [say], this might work."[5]

It was Lin's first away game since the start of his success, yet the Verizon Center somehow housed a significant number of New York fans – or perhaps everyone was a Lin fan that day. The chants and cheers for Lin must have made the home team crowd nervous. They seemed outnumbered on their own turf. Distance could not stifle the shouts of "Linsanity!" Jeremy was hoping to continue his streak.

Team dynamics had connected seamlessly. Lin was able to break the Wizard's defense and cut to the basket over and over. He found shooters and chucked balls outside the paint and sometimes even beyond the arc. Lin's mastery was in understanding each player's position as well as his own. The most successful approach was team-based, not superstar-centric, and Lin understood that. Still, he finished with a double-double – 23 points and 10 assists – an NBA career first for the young man.

Lin's showmanship did not disappoint the crowd. In the third quarter, for example, he took off on an "unexpected driving dunk that gave the Knicks a 72-66 lead and brought the fans out of their seats."[6] In classic humble fashion, Lin wrote the move off, telling *The Washington Post*, it was "just one of those in-a-moment things. I think they messed up on their coverage, so I was able to get free."[7] By the end of the game, the crowd had turned on the home team, cheering Lin's every move. With Lin's leadership, the Knicks ended the game with a 107-93 victory.

* * *

By now, the epidemic had become widespread. "Linsanity" had spread across America, Asia, Australia,

Europe, and Africa. Lin was now a global force whose journey had inspired millions across the planet. His story amazed people the world over. Was it that he was breaking barriers and expectations for Asian basketball players? Or perhaps that he had majored in Economics at Harvard? Maybe it was the fact that he had failed to receive any offers from Division 1 schools, went undrafted after Harvard, and bounced around from franchise to franchise, with stops in the D-League along the way? Were individuals taken by the power of his faith? Or did people just love a good underdog story, whose title character was played by a humble, hard working 23-year-old who had been giving his all his entire life? Whatever the answer, it was clear that in some way Jeremy Lin had ushered in a new era of sports fandom. And it was only the beginning.

In just a few short days, Jeremy Lin's name had become ever-present. His photos were splashed across the major newspapers and magazines. *SportsCenter* was running Jeremy Lin programming throughout the day. Paparazzi and media outlets were stalking Lin's family in Taiwan, including his paternal grandmother who had helped raise him.

Commentators, pundits, newscasters, reporters, comedians, coaches, and just about everyone else was preoccupied with constructing their latest "Lin" pun – Linsane, Linderella Story, Just 'Lin Time, Linsurrection, Linterplanetary, Lincalculable, Lincarnation, and the list goes on and on.

Sporting goods stores quickly sold out of Lin jerseys, while t-shirt vendors failed to keep up with the demand of Lin souvenirs. Women were even proposing to Lin on YouTube! Ben & Jerry's released a "Lin-Sanity" frozen yogurt flavor. Even President Obama commended Jeremy's triumph.

But it was as if the hype did not affect Jeremy.[8] He was certainly overwhelmed and grateful for the support, but he remained the simple, God-loving, humble kid he had always been.

After "Linsanity" rocked the nation, former Harvard roommate Eric Lee called Jeremy to congratulate him on his success. In true Lin fashion, Jeremy turned the conversation around on Lee. "It was never about him. The last thing he wanted to talk about was basketball or himself," Lee told *The Harvard Crimson*. "He wanted to hear about us."[9]

* * *

February 10, 2012 – New York Knicks vs. Los Angeles Lakers

Heading into the February 10 Lakers-Knicks match-up, Kobe Bryant claimed he did not know who Jeremy Lin was. He told a throng of probing reporters, "I don't even know what he's done. Like, I have no idea what you guys are talking about. I'll take a look at [the tape] tonight though."[10]   Regardless, Bryant quickly learned just who Jeremy Lin was. Nor would he ever forget.

Lin once again dominated at Madison Square Garden – his new, rightfully earned home. Lin led the Knicks to a 92-85 victory, achieving a career high (for the third time in a week and a half) of 38 points with 4 rebounds, 7 assists and 2 steals. His game-play was dynamic – he was explosive in the lane, took to the basket aggressively, yet ran the floor like a well-oiled machine. Every pass seemed choreographed, every basket effortless. The Knicks expanded their winning streak to four, and Lin proved to the world that he was no one-week wonder. He was here to stay and he was a force to be reckoned with.

"Lin #17" jerseys filled the Garden, while fans chanted "MVP! MVP!" for the electric point guard.[11] A new aura swept the arena. Confidence, excitement, and gratitude exuded from the Knicks faithful. They had witnessed a phenomenon and they loved what they saw. Coach D'Antoni expressed his exhilaration to *The New York Times*: "You don't see many guys play like that, even in their 30th opportunity, their whole career," D'Antoni said. "What he's doing is amazing."[12]

Lin was not one to be swept up by the insanity. He saw the game as another consistent effort by a selfless team. "I didn't try to see this game as any different," Lin told *ESPN*. "I just try to make sure that when I get there on the floor, I play as hard as I can and try to do everything I can to help the team win. The only thing we established tonight is four in a row. Now we try to go for five tomorrow. I'm not too worried about proving anything to anybody. As a team we're growing and trying to build on the momentum."[13]

Just a week ago, Lin had been nothing more than an afterthought. The twice-cut point guard had never started in an NBA game and had hardly done much damage when given the opportunity. Now, he was the stuff of a worldwide movement. If Kobe Bryant hadn't known him before, this was an incredible introduction. Even Bryant couldn't deny the holding power the Lin exuded. "I think it's a great story," Bryant later told *The New York Times*. "It's a testament to perseverance and hard work, and I think a good example for kids everywhere."[14]

February 11, 2012 – February 28, 2012

The following evening, on February 11, Lin and the Knicks were at the Target Center in Minneapolis, readying for a bout against the Timberwolves. Lin's shooting percentage took a hit, going 1 for 12 in the field, though he still worked the team expertly and managed 20 points and 8 assists by the end of the game. His pick-and-rolls worked well as he led the team in an impressive first half, and sought a bit more support in the second. But, as usual, his Knicks teammates delivered, keeping the lead and finally sealing the deal. A crucial free-throw with under 5 seconds remaining secured a 100-98 victory, the team's fifth-straight.

On Valentine's Day, the Knicks met the Raptors in Toronto. It seemed that Lin kept getting better with each game. Yet again, the opposing team's crowd was feeling the "Linsanity." The reception at the Air Canada Centre was overwhelming for the 23-year-old. Every basket or assist warranted an overpowering bellow from the crowd, which was excited to get a taste of Lin's talents.

It was another incredible team showing, with Shumpert and Stoudemire holding their own against the

Raptors. The Knicks kept pace with Toronto, though with less than two minutes on the clock they were trailing 87-82. Shumpert reduced the deficit with a dunk, followed by a three-pointer from Lin. The game was tied with a minute to play.

After two missed baskets from each team and five seconds on the clock, Lin drove in and released a shot from behind the arc. It was to be the shot heard round the world! The game-winning 3-pointer catapulted the Knicks to a sixth straight victory. Lin scored 27 points, 11 assists, 2 rebounds, and 1 steal. He had just set a record in the NBA, having scored more points in his five first starts – 136 – than any other player.[15] Linsanity was unstoppable!

The next seven games continued to display Lin's strengths. Though the Knicks recorded three losses before the end of February – against the New Orleans Hornets, the New Jersey Nets, and the Miami Heat – they had become a viable team, with a renewed capacity for greatness. For his part, Lin scored 26 points against New Orleans, 28 against the Mavericks, 21 in New Jersey, and 19 in Cleveland. For the month of February Lin averaged 20.9 points per game, 35.1 minutes of playing time, 8.4 assists, 4 rebounds, and 2.1 steals.[16]

But aside from his impressive statistics, Lin had

turned around a losing basketball franchise. He showed millions across the country that hard work and perseverance can get you places. He proved to millions of Asians and Asian-Americans that race should not limit people from doing what they love. He returned the NBA to its glory days by affirming that a team should be valued more than its star. But most of all, he offered to New York, the nation, and the world, a simple story. If you believe in yourself, and you work hard, anything is possible.

Yes! I have a raging case of Linsanity. I have been declared legally Linsane. My symptoms.. linsomnia, restless linsyndrome and lintestinal blockage!

— **Stephen Colbert,** *The Colbert Report*

EPILOGUE

On August 23, 1988, Gie-Ming and Shirley Lin welcomed a baby boy into the world who served as a symbol and fulfillment of their American Dream. That boy would grow up with a dream of his own – a dream that seemed unlikely at times, impossible at others.

Jeremy wanted to play in the NBA. It had been his dream since before he could remember. And he couldn't seem to shake that feeling. Though the odds were stacked against him, though it would have been easier on so many occasions to quit, he didn't.

It was as simple as that: not giving up. Twenty-three years would pass from that sweltering August day until that child's dream would finally become a reality. But while the dream had been simply making it to the NBA, no one – not even Jeremy himself – could have imagined the reality that he would soon be living.

It is an unlikely story. It is a tale of a father who fell in love with a sport he had never played, who trained himself in the image of the greats, and who passed that love and knowledge onto his three sons. It is the journey of a mother who devoted so much of herself to her son's true passion, always finding new opportunities to help him pursue his dream. It is the saga of a scrappy, skinny, 5-foot-3 Asian-American who defied racial stereotypes and size disadvantages to become a dominant force on the court. It is a story of fearless coaches who inspired commitment and respect, and rewarded a hunger to learn. It is a story of rejection, of adapting to circumstances, of tackling challenges, and finding hope in the hopeless.

Jeremy's journey is a modern-day David and Goliath tale. Through faith, family, and an ironclad will, Jeremy battled the odds to reach his goals. In the process, he also became a worldwide phenomenon, inspiring hope in millions of people across the world.

But what started "Linsanity?" Why did people the world over tune in, buy jerseys, make posters, write stories, even cook up a new ice cream flavor? Why did people pay attention? The answer seems to reside in the simplicity of Lin's story: the journey of a boy who followed his dream and opened up a world of possibility.

Though it was years in the making, Jeremy's success on the court, in the matter of a few short weeks, has created a lasting legacy. His achievement has encouraged an entire continent – and individuals of Asian descent everywhere – that race is not and should never be a factor in achieving one's dreams.

More specifically, Lin has changed the way that coaches, recruiters, managers and others will view athletes of Asian-American descent. His success is a call to young Asian-American athletes everywhere that race and culture don't have anything to do with athletic success. It seems that this may finally be a tipping point in amateur and professional athletics, as prejudice is washed away at the high school, college, and professional levels.

Jeremy's success will also help aid the transformation of Harvard men's basketball into a nationally competitive program. Jeremy's rise will serve as proof that playing at Harvard can lead to a professional career.

Coach Tommy Amaker acknowledges the "Lin Factor" in an interview with *ESPN* saying "What [Jeremy] was able to do while he was here [was] kind of establish an identity with this program. Jeremy was as big as any piece of the puzzle for us to start the music."[1]

Jeremy's stardom gives Harvard basketball unique credibility. Already there are hints that a number of nationally ranked high school players have honed in on the Harvard recruitment process for this year. If nothing else, Lin's time at Harvard and his post-graduate legacy has made basketball a more popular sport on campus.

"Linsanity" will also undoubtedly change the way the NBA looks at its players. Already, owners and general managers, coaches and trainers are combing their reserves, D-Leagues, and benches to see whether they may have another superstar-in-waiting.

Lin's exploits were made possible by many factors – two injured powerhouse players, a lack of effective point guards, and an act of desperation from Mike D'Antoni. His strengths and talents were not immediately evident from 3-on-3 pre-draft workouts or practice drills. He needed the opportunity to play the game as it was meant to be played – 5-on-5 – in order to shine.

But most of all, Jeremy's journey sends a message about underdogs everywhere. His story serves as an example that we can all fulfill our dreams. If we believe in ourselves, work hard, and stay focused, we all have the capacity to achieve great things. It is not every day that one individual's success story translates across languages and religions, cultures and races, to captivate an entire planet. Jeremy Lin inspires the best in all of us, as he reminds us of what ties us all together as human beings – love, family, faith, and dreams.

Jeremy wasn't looking to change the world. He just wanted a chance to play some ball. Along the way, he inspired millions, sparked a phenomenon and reminded all of us of what really matters. It is a long way from that sweltering August in 1988. But once again, it is the year of the Underdog. And today, something special is in the air.

"I haven't done a computation, but it's fair to say that no player has created the interest and the frenzy in this short period of time, in any sport, that I'm aware of like Jeremy Lin has."

— NBA Commissioner David Stern

LOOK WHO'S TALKING

"I've been on the Jeremy Lin bandwagon for a while…
I can't take credit for it, but I'm just saying I was there
early."

> **—President Barack Obama, on learning about
> Lin when the Knicks point guard was still a
> senior at Harvard**

"It's a great story, and what's interesting is the fact that
somehow folks were missing it in practice…"

> **—President Barack Obama**

"It's a terrific story, [Jeremy] seems like a wonderful
young man, and it elevates this great sport all around
the world."

> **—President Barack Obama**

"I haven't done a computation, but it's fair to say that
no player has created the interest and the frenzy in this
short period of time, in any sport, that I'm aware of like
Jeremy Lin has."

> **— NBA Commissioner David Stern**

"I think this is why we all follow sports, because of great stories like [Jeremy's], that all of a sudden someone breaks through that you did not know or didn't expect and you didn't know the result was going to happen. And that he was able to help the Knicks to come through in the way he did now is a great thing."

— Tennis great Roger Federer

"[Jeremy Lin] does what needs to be done. If they need scoring, he provides that. He's very unselfish; once he gets inside he's looking to pass the ball. But when there's an opportunity to let him score he's doing that as well. He's just unflappable. It's amazing that a guy has no experience, coming into the NBA been cut by 3 or 4 teams that he can find his niche seemingly overnight. And how he's rejuvenated this franchise."

**—Walt Frazier, former Knick and
NBA Hall-of-Famer**

"I think it's a great story. It's a testament to perseverance and hard work, and I think a good example for kids everywhere."

> **—Kobe Bryant after Lin outscored him 38-31 in a Knicks win.**

"Yes! I have a raging case of Linsanity. I have been declared legally Linsane. My symptoms.. linsomnia, restless linsyndrome and lintestinal blockage!"

> **—Stephen Colbert, The Colbert Report**

"What I see from Jeremy and what I hear in his interviews is he appreciates everything. He pursues his dream. His attitude is so peaceful, but there is strength to him. It is not a violent strength like fire or something aggressive. It is like the ocean, very peaceful, very quiet when you look at it. But you can never underestimate the power that is in there."

> **—Yao Ming**

"His basketball IQ, his ability to know what play to run, what pass to make, how to run the pick-and-roll or a stutter-step to hold the defense, that's stuff you can't teach. He's also got that swagger and that confidence that you need to be successful on the basketball court."

—Magic Johnson

"Linsanity. Wow. What a run. You look at the Giants, you look at Linsanity and there's been so many great things happening in New York. We kind of feel like we want to jump in the party. The great thing about Linsanity is that, it kind of reminds you of how fun the game should be. For some of us that have been playing for a long time, it's just the one second you take the game for granted, it makes you realize how much fun the game is."

—Alex Rodriguez, New York Yankees

"I knew him before he was Linmania. He's still the same humble guy. The guy has not changed a bit, which is real special for a young man."

—Keith Smart, Sacramento Kings coach

"Don't try to explain it, dissect it. We're just in the middle of it and enjoy it. Especially if you are a Knick fan… It's a great American story. A great American story."

—Spike Lee, when asked about Linsanity

BIBLIOGRAPHY

Bibliography

CHAPTER 1

i "Prospect Profile: Jeremy Lin." NBA.com. 2010. Web. 03 Mar. 2012.
<http://www.nba.com/draft2010/prospects/jeremy-lin/>.

ii Borden, Sam, and Keith Bradsher. "Tight-Knit Family Shares Lin's Achievement." The

New York Times 26 Feb. 2012, New York ed.: SP1. New York Times. 25 Feb. 2012.
Web.

2 Mar. 2012.

iii Ibid.

iv Ibid.

v Ibid.

vi Ibid.

vii Ibid.

viii O'Neil, Dana. "Immigrant Dream Plays out through Son." ESPN.com. ESPN,
10 Dec.

2009. Web. 29 Feb. 2012.

ix Ibid.

x Ibid.

xi Ibid.

xii Ibid.

xiii Ibid.

xiv Borden, Sam, and Keith Bradsher. "Tight-Knit Family Shares Lin's Achievement." The

New York Times 26 Feb. 2012, New York ed.: SP1. New York Times. 25 Feb. 2012.
Web.

2 Mar. 2012.

xv Ibid.

xvi Ibid.

xvii Ibid.

xviii O'Neil, Dana. "Immigrant Dream Plays out through Son." ESPN.com. ESPN,
10 Dec.

2009. Web. 29 Feb. 2012.

xix Ibid.

xx Ibid.

xxi Ibid.

xxii Ibid.

xxiii Ibid.

xxiv Ibid.

xxv Branch, Eric. "Jeremy Lin's Rise from Ordinary Guy to Sensation." San
Francisco

Chronicle 23 Feb. 2012: A1. Print.

xxvi Borden, Sam, and Keith Bradsher. "Tight-Knit Family Shares Lin's Achievement."

The New York Times 26 Feb. 2012, New York ed.: SP1. New York Times. 25 Feb.
2012.

Web. 2 Mar. 2012.

xxvii Ibid.

xxviii Keown, Tim. "Jeremy Lin's HS coach is surprised, too." ESPN.com. ESPN,
14 Feb.

2012. Web. 28 Feb. 2012.

xxix Ghadishah, Arash. "Jeremy Lin's High-School Coach Recalls a Star on the
Rise." The

Daily Beast. 18 Feb. 2012. Web. 25 Feb. 2012.

xxx Chandler, Rick. "Rick' ™s Cafe: Early Signs of Linsanity... Jeremy Lin Was Something Special from the Very start." Off the Bench. NBC Sports, 09 Feb. 2012. Web.

03 Mar. 2012. <http://offthebench.nbcsports.com/2012/02/09/ricks-cafe-early-signs-oflinsanity-

jeremy-lin-was-something-special-from-the-very-start/>.

xxxi Ibid.

xxxii Ibid.

xxxiii Parsons, Tim. "Former Tahoe Scribe Was Lin's Middle-school Coach." North Lake

Tahoe Bonanza. 22 Feb. 2012. Web. 4 Mar. 2012.

xxxiv Dalrymple, Timothy. "Jeremy Lin, Faith, and Ethnicity." Patheos.com. 04 Mar.

2010. Web. 02 Mar. 2012.

CHAPTER 2

i Torre, Pablo S. "From Couch to Clutch." Sports Illustrated 20 Feb. 2012. SportsIllustrated.com. 20 Feb. 2012. Web. 26 Feb. 2012.

ii Tseng, Katie. "Weekly One-on-One: Jeremy Lin." The Paly Voice. 6 Mar. 2005. Web.

27 Feb. 2012.

iii O'Neil, Dana. "Immigrant Dream Plays out through Son." ESPN.com. ESPN, 10 Dec.

2009. Web. 29 Feb. 2012.

iv "Jeremy Lin Was a Surprise Star in High School, Too." Rivals High. Yahoo! Sports, 17

Feb. 2012. Web. 04 Mar. 2012.

<http://highschool.rivals.com/content.asp?CID=1332411>.

v Meuel, Jimmy. "Winter Sports Teams Compete in CCS Playoffs." The Campanile. The

Paly Voice, 10 Mar. 2003. Web. 27 Feb. 2012.

vi Ibid.

vii Balamane, Nabil. " Boys' basketball loses heartbreaker in CCS." The Paly Voice. 1

Mar. 2004. Web. 27 Feb. 2012.

viii Spander, Art. "Jeremy Lin Leaves Warriors Wondering 'What If?'" San Francisco

Examiner. 14 Feb. 2012. Web. 02 Mar. 2012.

ix Tseng, Katie. "Weekly One-on-One: Jeremy Lin." The Paly Voice. 6 Mar. 2005. Web.

27 Feb. 2012.

x Ibid.

xi Coughan, David. "Winter athletic teams prepare for upcoming seasons." The Campanile. The Paly Voice, 24 Nov. 2003. Web. 28 Feb. 2012.

xii Ghadishah, Arash. "Jeremy Lin's High-School Coach Recalls a Star on the Rise." The

Daily Beast. 18 Feb. 2012. Web. 25 Feb. 2012.

xiii Balamane, Nabil. "Excessive fouls plague boys' basketball team." The Paly Voice. 14

Jan. 2004. Web. 01 Mar. 2012.

xiv Balamane, Nabil. "Vikings bruise Santa Clara Bruins." The Paly Voice. 30 Jan. 2004.

Web. 01 Mar. 2012.

xv Schulte, Sara. "Viking hoops off to roaring start in CCS." The Campanile. The Paly

Voice, 1 Mar. 2004. Web. 27 Feb. 2012.

xvi Ibid.

xvii Ibid.

xviii Ibid.

xix Balamane, Nabil. " Boys' basketball loses heartbreaker in CCS." The Paly Voice. 1

Mar. 2004. Web. 27 Feb. 2012.

xx Torre, Pablo S. "From Couch to Clutch." Sports Illustrated 20 Feb. 2012. SportsIllustrated.com. 20 Feb. 2012. Web. 26 Feb. 2012.

xxi Branch, Eric. "Jeremy Lin's Rise from Ordinary Guy to Sensation." San Francisco

Chronicle 23 Feb. 2012: A1. Print.

xxii Ghadishah, Arash. "Jeremy Lin's High-School Coach Recalls a Star on the Rise." The

Daily Beast. 18 Feb. 2012. Web. 25 Feb. 2012.

xxiii Lin, Jeremy. "Paly tennis struggles." The Campanile. The Paly Voice, 10 Oct. 2005.

Web. 28 Feb. 2012.

xxiv Barich, Katie. "Faith-based clubs take different approaches to religion." The

Campanile. The Paly Voice, 21 Nov. 2005. Web. 28 Feb. 2012.

xxv Borden, Sam, and Keith Bradsher. "Tight-Knit Family Shares Lin's Achievement."

The New York Times 26 Feb. 2012, New York ed.: SP1. New York Times. 25 Feb. 2012.

Web. 4 Mar. 2012.

xxvi Burke, Daniel. "New York Knicks' Jeremy Lin Dubbed the "Taiwanese Tebow""

Religion News Service. 14 Feb. 2012. Web. 24 Feb. 2012. <http://www.religionnews.com/culture/sports/new-york-knicks-guard-dubbed-thetaiwanese-

tebow>.

xxvii Narciso, Gerald. "We Reminisce: Jeremy Lin's First Appearance in Dime Magazine."

Dime Magazine. 15 Feb. 2012. Web. 25 Feb. 2012.

xxviii O'Neil, Dana. "Immigrant Dream Plays out through Son." ESPN.com. ESPN, 10

Dec. 2009. Web. 29 Feb. 2012.

xxix Narciso, Gerald. "We Reminisce: Jeremy Lin's First Appearance in Dime Magazine."

Dime Magazine. 15 Feb. 2012. Web. 25 Feb. 2012.

xxx Steinman, Jonathan. "Boys' basketball destroys early season competitors." The

Campanile. The Paly Voice, 17 Dec. 2004. Web. 28 Feb. 2012.

xxxi Thompson, Maggie. "Boys' basketball shoots for league perfection." The Campanile.

The Paly Voice, 14 Feb. 2005. Web. 29 Feb. 2012.

xxxii Shaikh, Huda. "Paly basketball sweeps at Gunn, with varsity boys dominating, 69-

27." The Paly Voice. 7 Feb. 2005. Web. 27 Feb. 2012.

xxxiii Thompson, Maggie. "Boys' basketball shoots for league perfection." The Campanile.

The Paly Voice, 14 Feb. 2005. Web. 29 Feb. 2012.

xxxiv Ferber, Richie. "Boys Basketball team dominates Sequoia to move on to Semifinals."

The Paly Voice. 5 Mar. 2005. Web. 27 Feb. 2012.

xxxv Lefebvre, David. "Boys' basketball aims for State title, girls eliminated." The

Campanile. The Paly Voice, 7 Mar. 2005. Web. 28 Feb. 2012.

xxxvi Ibid.

xxxvii Kelman, Jake. "Boys basketball team triumphs in CCS but falters in NorCal finals."

The Campanile. The Paly Voice, 25 Mar. 2005. Web. 28 Feb. 2012.

xxxviii Heeger, Adam. "Boys' basketball dominates Chico, moves to NorCal finals." The

Paly Voice. 10 Mar. 2005. Web. 28 Feb. 2012.

xxxix Kelman, Jake. "Boys basketball team triumphs in CCS but falters in NorCal finals."

The Campanile. The Paly Voice, 25 Mar. 2005. Web. 28 Feb. 2012.

xl Serby, Steve. "Serby's Q&A with … Jeremy Lin." New York Post. 18 Feb. 2012. Web.

3 Mar. 2012.

xli Keown, Tim. "Jeremy Lin's HS coach is surprised, too." ESPN.com. ESPN, 14 Feb.

2012. Web. 28 Feb. 2012.

xlii Steinman, Jonathan. "Boys' basketball on smooth ride, girls beginning to gel." The

Campanile. The Paly Voice, 16 Dec. 2005. Web. 28 Feb. 2012.

xliii Ibid.

xliv Schwartz, Carey and Siddhartha Oza. "Paly basketball records seventh straight victory, stays unbeaten." The Paly Voice. 13 Dec. 2005. Web. 28 Feb. 2012.

xlv Schwartz, Carey and Siddhartha Oza. "Viking basketball on top from start to finish."

The Paly Voice. 04 Feb. 2006. Web. 28 Feb. 2012.

xlvi Ibid.

xlvii Ibid.

xlviii Sondheimer, Eric. "Another Upset Hits Mater Dei." Los Angeles Times. 18 Mar.

2006. Web. 22 Feb. 2012.

xlix Schwartz, Carey and Siddhartha Oza. "Viking basketball on top from start to finish."

The Paly Voice. 04 Feb. 2006. Web. 28 Feb. 2012.

l Sondheimer, Eric. "Another Upset Hits Mater Dei." Los Angeles Times. 18 Mar. 2006.

Web. 22 Feb. 2012.

li Ibid.

lii Schwartz, Carey and Siddhartha Oza. "Viking's achieve perfect ending to a perfect

season." The Paly Voice. 18 Mar. 2006. Web. 28 Feb. 2012.

liii Ibid.

liv Ghadishah, Arash. "Jeremy Lin's High-School Coach Recalls a Star on the Rise." The

Daily Beast. 18 Feb. 2012. Web. 25 Feb. 2012.

lv Thompson, Maggie. "Senior standouts lead Paly athletics to triumph." The Campanile.

The Paly Voice, 5 Jun. 2006. Web. 28 Feb. 2012.

lv The Campanile Editorial Staff. "Athletes of the Year." The Campanile. The Paly Voice,

5 Jun. 2006. Web. 28 Feb. 2012.

lvii Lin, Jeremy. "Jeremy Lin: My Reflection On Our State Championship." The Paly

Voice. 15 Feb. 2012. Web. 24 Feb. 2012.

CHAPTER 3

i "Q&A with Jeremy Lin." Interview. SFGate.com. San Francisco Chronicle, 22 July

2010. Web. 22 Feb. 2012.

ii Bolch, Ben. "Jeremy Lin's High School Coach Says Race Hindered Opportunities." Los

Angeles Times. 17 Feb. 2012. Web. 8 Mar. 2012.

iii Tseng, Katie. "Weekly One-on-One: Jeremy Lin." The Paly Voice. 6 Mar. 2005. Web.

27 Feb. 2012.

iv Torre, Pablo S. "Harvard School of Basketball." Sports Illustrated 01 Feb. 2010. SportsIllustrated.com. 01 Feb. 2012. Web. 26 Feb. 2012.

v Bolch, Ben. "Jeremy Lin's High School Coach Says Race Hindered Opportunities." Los

Angeles Times. 17 Feb. 2012. Web. 8 Mar. 2012.

vi Ibid.

vii Viera, Mark. "For Lin, Erasing a History of Being Overlooked." New York Times. 12

Feb. 2012. Web. 5 Mar. 2012.

viii Torre, Pablo S. "Harvard School of Basketball." Sports Illustrated 01 Feb. 2010. SportsIllustrated.com. 01 Feb. 2012. Web. 26 Feb. 2012.

ix Viera, Mark. "For Lin, Erasing a History of Being Overlooked." New York Times. 12

Feb. 2012. Web. 5 Mar. 2012.

x Torre, Pablo S. "Harvard School of Basketball." Sports Illustrated 01 Feb. 2010. SportsIllustrated.com. 01 Feb. 2012. Web. 26 Feb. 2012.

xi Viera, Mark. "For Lin, Erasing a History of Being Overlooked." New York Times. 12

Feb. 2012. Web. 5 Mar. 2012.

xii Zagoria, Adam. "Coach Says Jeremy Lin Was Misled By Stanford Coach." Web log

post. ZagsBlog. 10 Feb. 2012. Web. 6 Mar. 2012.

xiii Ibid.

xiv Ibid.

xv Ibid.

xvi Ibid.

xvii "Q&A with Jeremy Lin." Interview. SFGate.com. San Francisco Chronicle, 22 July

2010. Web. 22 Feb. 2012.

xviii Viera, Mark. "For Lin, Erasing a History of Being Overlooked." New York Times. 12

Feb. 2012. Web. 5 Mar. 2012.

xix Ibid.

xx Ibid.

Bibliography

CHAPTER 4

i Zheng, Dennis J. "GAME OF THE YEAR: Buzzer-Beater Gives Crimson Triple-Overtime Win." The Harvard Crimson. 27 May 2010. Web. 27 Feb. 2012.

ii Zheng, Dennis J. "Lin's Triple-Overtime Shot Gives Harvard Thrilling Win." The Harvard Crimson. 16 Nov. 2009. Web. 27 Feb. 2012.

iii Ibid.

iv Ibid.

v "Jeremy Lin." Men's Basketball. Go Crimson: Harvard Athletics. Web. 22 Feb. 2012.

<http://www.gocrimson.com/sports/mbkb/2009-10/bios/Jeremy_Lin_Bio>.

vi Tang, Dennis. "Jeremy Lin: "He's a Lot Like Tim Tebow"" GQ 13 Feb. 2012. GQ.com.

13 Feb. 2012. Web. 2 Mar. 2012.

vii Hamlin, Tucker. "Mr. Reddicks and Jeremy Lin." The Milton Measure. 24 Feb. 2012.

Web. 28 Feb. 2012. <http://miltonmeasure.org/2012/02/mr-reddicks-and-jeremy-lin/>.

viii "Jeremy Lin." Men's Basketball. Go Crimson: Harvard Athletics. Web. 22 Feb. 2012.

<http://www.gocrimson.com/sports/mbkb/2009-10/bios/Jeremy_Lin_Bio>.

ix Ibid.

x Ibid.

xi Ibid.

xii Armstrong, Kevin. "The True Hollywood Story of the Knick Linsation." New York

Daily News. 11 Feb. 2012. Web. 21 Feb. 2012.

xiii Dortch, Chris. "Harvard Was Perfect Place for Lin to Hone Guard Skills." NBA.com.

17 Feb. 2012. Web. 3 Mar. 2012.

xiv Ibid.

xv Ibid.

xvi "Jeremy Lin." Men's Basketball. Go Crimson: Harvard Athletics. Web. 22 Feb. 2012.

<http://www.gocrimson.com/sports/mbkb/2009-10/bios/Jeremy_Lin_Bio>.

xvii Ibid.

xviii Ibid.

xix Ibid.

xx Ibid.

xxi Gryboski, Michael. "Jeremy Lin Was Bible Study Teacher at Harvard University."

Christian Post. 17 Feb. 2012. Web. 28 Feb. 2012.

<http://www.christianpost.com/news/jeremy-lin-was-bible-study-teacher-at-harvarduniversity-

69767/>

xxii Ibid.

xxiii Ibid.

xxiv Ibid.

xxv Feldman, Jacob D.H. "Lin Has Friends, Faith to Thank for Success." The Harvard

Crimson. 22 Feb. 2012. Web. 27 Feb. 2012.

xxvi Ibid.

xxvii O'Neil, Dana. "Immigrant Dream Plays out through Son." ESPN.com. ESPN,

Bibliography

10 Dec.

2009. Web. 29 Feb. 2012.

xxviii Ibid.

xxix Kirby, Ted. "Men's Basketball Stund No.17 Boston College, 82-70." The Harvard

Crimson. 08 Jan. 2009. Web. 28 Feb. 2012.

xxx Ibid.

xxxi Ibid.

xxxii Ibid.

xxxiii "Jeremy Lin." Men's Basketball. Go Crimson: Harvard Athletics. Web. 22 Feb. 2012.

<http://www.gocrimson.com/sports/mbkb/2009-10/bios/Jeremy_Lin_Bio>.

xxxiv Ibid.

xxxv Ibid.

xxxvi Ibid.

xxxvii Ibid.

xxxviii Dortch, Chris. "Harvard Was Perfect Place for Lin to Hone Guard Skills."

NBA.com. 17 Feb. 2012. Web. 3 Mar. 2012.

xxxix Ibid.

xl Zheng, Dennis J. "GAME OF THE YEAR: Buzzer-Beater Gives Crimson Triple-Overtime Win." The Harvard Crimson. 27 May 2010. Web. 27 Feb. 2012.

xli Ibid.

xlii Zheng, Dennis J. "Lin's Triple-Overtime Shot Gives Harvard Thrilling Win." The

Harvard Crimson. 16 Nov. 2009. Web. 27 Feb. 2012.

xliii Ibid.

xliv Kistler, Emmett. "Harvard Hangs Tight With No.13 UConn." The Harvard Crimson.

07 Dec. 2009. Web. 28 Feb. 2012.xlv Ibid.

xlvi Ibid.

xlvii Ibid.

xlviii Ibid.

xlix "Jeremy Lin." Men's Basketball. Go Crimson: Harvard Athletics. Web. 22 Feb. 2012.

<http://www.gocrimson.com/sports/mbkb/2009-10/bios/Jeremy_Lin_Bio>.l Ibid.

li Ibid.

lii Ibid.

liii Ibid.

liv Zheng, Dennis J. "GAME OF THE YEAR: Buzzer-Beater Gives Crimson Triple-Overtime Win." The Harvard Crimson. 27 May 2010. Web. 27 Feb. 2012.

lv Zimmerman, Jonathan. "In Jeremy Lin, a Stereotype That Should Be Celebrated." The

Washington Post. 16 Feb. 2012. Web. 5 Mar. 2012.

CHAPTER 5

i "Harvard Alum Jeremy Lin Talks about the Crimson's Big Weekend." The Boston Herald. 4 Mar. 2012. Web. 5 Mar. 2012.

ii Ibid.

iii Culpepper, Chuck. "An All-Around Talent, Obscured by His Pedigree." The New York

Bibliography

Times. 14 Sept. 2010. Web. 4 Mar. 2012.

iv Ibid.

v Garcia, Art. "Why Mavericks, NBA Didn't Catch Linsanity Earlier." Fort Worth Star

Telegram. 18 Feb. 2012. Web. 4 Mar. 2012.

vi Culpepper, Chuck. "An All-Around Talent, Obscured by His Pedigree." The New York

Times. 14 Sept. 2010. Web. 4 Mar. 2012.

vii Stein, Marc. "Jeremy Lin Added to Rising Stars game." ESPN.com. 17 Feb. 2012.

Web. 04 Mar. 2012.

viii Kessler, Martin. "Jeremy Lin to Sign With Warriors, Reports Say." The Harvard Crimson. 20 Jul. 2010. Web. 27 Feb. 2012.

ix Stein, Marc. "Jeremy Lin Added to Rising Stars game." ESPN.com. 17 Feb. 2012. Web.

04 Mar. 2012.

x Culpepper, Chuck. "An All-Around Talent, Obscured by His Pedigree." The New York

Times. 14 Sept. 2010. Web. 4 Mar. 2012.

xi Garcia, Art. "Why Mavericks, NBA Didn't Catch Linsanity Earlier." Fort Worth Star

Telegram. 18 Feb. 2012. Web. 4 Mar. 2012.

xii Ibid.

xiii Beck, Howard. "Newest Knick Out to Prove He's Not Just a Novelty." The New York

Times. 28 Dec. 2011. Web. 28 Feb. 2012.

xiv Hughes, Frank. "Former Harvard standout Lin ready to prove himself with Warriros."

Sports Illustrated 26 Jul. 2012. SportsIllustrated.com. Web. 26 Feb. 2012.

xv "Stop cheering for Jeremy Lin." SFGate.com. San Francisco Chronicle, 2 Nov. 2010.

Web. 22 Feb. 2012.

xvi "Jeremy Lin Sent to NBA D-League." Web log post. Channel APA: Broadcasting

Asian America. 28 Dec. 2010. Web. 28 Feb. 2012.

<http://www.channelapa.com/2010/12/jeremy-lin-sent-to-nba-d-league.html>.

xvii Beck, Howard. "The Evolution of a Point Guard." The New York Times. 24 Feb. 2012.

Web. 2 Mar. 2012.

xviii Ibid.

xix Ibid.

xx Ibid.

xxi Brown, Daniel. "Bay Area Trainers Helped Make Knicks Guard Jeremy Lin Better,

Stronger, Faster." San Jose Mercury News. 24 Feb. 2012. Web. 4 Mar. 2012.

xxii Ibid.

xxiii Ibid.

xxiv Ibid.

xxv Ibid.

xxvi Ibid.

xxvii Ibid.

xxviii Beck, Howard. "The Evolution of a Point Guard." The New York Times. 24

Feb.

2012. Web. 2 Mar. 2012.

xxix Ibid.

CHAPTER 6

i Garcia, Art. "Why Mavericks, NBA Didn't Catch Linsanity Earlier." Fort Worth Star.

Telegram. 18 Feb. 2012. Web. 4 Mar. 2012.

ii "Rockets sign rookie forward Morris." NBA.com. 12 Dec. 2011. Web. 03 Mar. 2012.

<http://www.nba.com/2011/news/12/12/rockets-morris.ap/index.html?rss=true/>.

iii Brown, Daniel. "Bay Area Trainers Helped Make Knicks Guard Jeremy Lin Better,

Stronger, Faster." San Jose Mercury News. 24 Feb. 2012. Web. 4 Mar. 2012.

iv Ibid.

v Ibid.

vi Begley, Ian. "Daryl Morey Regrets Jeremy Lin cut." ESPN.com. 09 Feb. 2012. Web. 04

Mar. 2012.

vii Feldman, Jacob D.H. "Lin Has Friends, Faith to Thank for Success." The Harvard

Crimson. 22 Feb. 2012. Web. 27 Feb. 2012.

viii Ibid.

ix Beck, Howard. "Lin's Success Surprising to Everyone." The New York Times. 9 Feb.

2012. Web. 28 Feb. 2012.

x Beck, Howard. "The Evolution of a Point Guard." The New York Times. 24 Feb. 2012.

Web. 2 Mar. 2012.

xi Beck, Howard. "Knicks' Strengths Vanish, and So Do Hopes of Winning." The New

York Times. 29 Dec. 2011. Web. 2 Mar. 2012.

xii Dickau, Adam. "The New York Knicks assign Jeremy Lin to the Erie Bay-Hawks."

Broke Jumper, 20 Jan. 2012. Web. 3 Mar. 2012.

xiii Zagoria, Adam. "Before the Knicks, Linsanity Reigned in the D-League." Web log

post. ZagsBlog. 13 Feb. 2012. Web. 4 Mar. 2012.

xiv Ibid.

xv Leitch, Will. "Recalling Lin's Game With the Erie BayHawks." New York Magazine.

14 Feb. 2012. Web. 8 Mar. 2012.

xvi Zagoria, Adam. "Before the Knicks, Linsanity Reigned in the D-League." Web log

post. ZagsBlog. 13 Feb. 2012. Web. 4 Mar. 2012.

xvii Ibid.

xviii Hughes, Luke. "Harvard's Tommy Amaker Proud of Jeremy Lin, Says He Is Ideal Fit

With Knicks." NESN.com. New England Sports Network, 14 Feb. 2012. Web. 1 Mar.

2012.

xix Ibid.

xx "Jeremy Lin: Game-by-Game Stats." ESPN.com. ESPN, 8 Mar. 2012, Web. 8

Bibliography

Mar.

2012.

xxi Deveney, Sean. "Frustrated D'Antoni Searching for Answers to Knicks' Problems."

Sporting News: NBA. AOL News, 05 Mar. 2012. Web. 06 Mar. 2012.

xxii Ibid.

CHAPTER 7

i "Nets vs. Knicks, 2/4/2012." ESPN.com. ESPN, 4 Feb. 2012, Web. 3 Mar. 2012. <http://scores.espn.go.com/nba/playbyplay?gameId=320204018&period=4>

ii Beck, Howard. "Lin Sparks Knicks, to Crowd's Delight and D'Antoni's Relief." The

New York Times. 4 Feb. 2012. Web. 28 Feb. 2012.

iii Ibid.

iv Ibid.

v "Jazz vs. Knicks, 2/6/2012." ESPN.com. ESPN, 6 Feb. 2012, Web. 3 Mar. 2012. <http://espn.go.com/nba/recap?gameId=320206018>

vi "Wizards vs. Knicks: Jeremy Lin and Tyson Chandler Outduel John Wall and Washington." The Washington Post. 09 Feb. 2012. Web. 02 Mar. 2012. <http://www.washingtonpost.com/wizards>.

vii Ibid.

viii Feldman, Jacob D.H. "Lin Has Friends, Faith to Thank for Success." The Harvard

Crimson. 22 Feb. 2012. Web. 27 Feb. 2012.

ix Ibid.

x Rohlin, Melissa. "Kobe Bryant Is Not Caught up in Jeremy Lin 'Linsanity'" The Los

Angeles Times Blog. 10 Feb. 2012. Web. 08 Mar. 2012. <http://latimesblogs.latimes.com/sports_blog/2012/02/kobe-bryant-comments-jeremylin.html>.

xi "Lakers vs. Knicks, 2/10/2012." ESPN.com. ESPN, 10 Feb. 2012, Web. 3 Mar. 2012.

<http://espn.go.com/nba/recap?gameId=320210018>

xii Beck, Howard. "With 38 Points, the Legend Grows." The New York Times. 10 Feb.

2012. Web. 28 Feb. 2012.

xiii "Lakers vs. Knicks, 2/10/2012." ESPN.com. ESPN, 10 Feb. 2012, Web. 3 Mar. 2012.

<http://espn.go.com/nba/recap?gameId=320210018>

xiv Beck, Howard. "With 38 Points, the Legend Grows." The New York Times. 10 Feb.

2012. Web. 28 Feb. 2012.

xv "Jeremy Lin: Game-by-Game Stats." ESPN.com. ESPN, 8 Mar. 2012, Web. 8 Mar.

2012.

xvi Ibid.

EPILOGUE

i McCluskey, Jack. "Jeremy Lin Gives Harvard Assist." ESPN Boston. 26 Feb. 2012.

Right Fit Reading

The mission of Right Fit Reading is to develop new content or repurpose old content that will help to improve reading levels. There is a significant reading problem in the United States and abroad today and there is a need for publishers to come up with better ways to ensure that we are getting the right books to the right readers. Right Fit Reading has developed a program that will create four different versions of books based on Lexile levels. Right Fit will be able to match our books to many more children. Right Fit Readers will be available in both paperback and eBook formats.